1000 things you should know about

prehistoric life

Andrew Campbell

Miles Kelly
PUBLISHING

This material was first published as hardback in 2005

This edition published in 2006 by Miles Kelly Publishing Ltd
Bardfield Centre, Great Bardfield, Essex, CM7 4SL

2 4 6 8 10 9 7 5 3 1

Editorial Director: Belinda Gallagher
Art Director: Jo Brewer
Volume Designer: Ian Paulyn
Additional Design: Candice Bekir
Picture Researcher Manager: Liberty Newton
Reprographics: Anthony Cambray, Mike Coupe,
Stephan Davis, Ian Paulyn

British Library Cataloguing-in-Publication Data
A catalogue record for this book is available from the British Library

ISBN 1-84236-695-5

Printed in China

info@mileskelly.net
www.mileskelly.net

All artworks are from the MKP Archives

All photographs from:
Castrol, CMCD, Corbis, Corel, digitalSTOCK, digitalvision, Flat Earth,
Hemera, ILN, John Foxx, PhotoAlto, PhotoDisc, PhotoEssentials,
PhotoPro, Stockbyte

1000 things you should know about

prehistoric life

CONTENTS

Prehistoric time

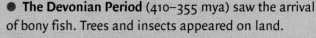

- **Time since Earth** formed is split into units called eras, which are in split into periods. Some periods split into epochs. These units relate to the formation of rock layers.

- **The Precambrian Era** ran from 4600–542 million years ago (mya). It saw the beginning of sea life. In the Cambrian Period (542–490 mya) vertebrates appeared.

- **In the Ordovician Period** (490–435 mya) plants spread to land. In the Silurian Period (435–410 mya) the first jawed fish appeared. Upright plants grew on land.

- **The Devonian Period** (410–355 mya) saw the arrival of bony fish. Trees and insects appeared on land.

- **The Carboniferous Period** (355–298 mya) was the time of great tropical forests and the first land vertebrates.

- **Reptiles ruled land** in the Permian Period (298–250 mya).

- **The Triassic Period** (250–208 mya) saw the rise of the dinosaurs and the first mammals. In the Jurassic Period (208–144 mya) reptiles ruled land, sea and sky.

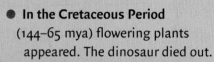

- **In the Cretaceous Period** (144–65 mya) flowering plants appeared. The dinosaur died out.

- **The Tertiary Period** (65–1.6 mya) saw the rise of mammals. Temperatures cooled.

- **The Quaternary Period** (1.6 mya–present) has seen the most recent ice ages and the rise of humans.

▼ Many animals and plants died out 65 mya, but other groups such as fish, insects, birds and mammals survived.

Earliest plants

- **The first living things** on Earth were single-celled bacteria and blue-green algae.

- **Blue-green algae** emerged around 3500 mya.

- **Although it is not a plant**, blue-green algae contains chlorophyll and was the first living thing to photosynthesize (make energy from sunlight).

- **Photosynthesis** also produces oxygen. Over millions of years, the blue-green algae produced enough oxygen to enable more complex life forms to develop.

- **True algae**, which are usually regarded as plants, developed around 1000 mya.

- **By about 550 mya**, multi-celled plants had begun to appear, including simple seaweeds.

◄ Lichens such as these are made up of an alga and fungus. Early lichens – like modern-day ones – grew on rocks and, over time, eroded part of the rock and helped form soil.

- **Algae and lichens** were the first plants to appear on land.

- **Bryophyte plants** (mosses and liverworts) emerged on land around 440 mya. Bryophytes are simple green seedless plants.

- **Bryophytes cannot grow high** above the ground because they do not have strengthened stems, unlike vascular plants, which emerged later.

★ STAR FACT ★
Liverworts grew on mats of blue-green algae, which trapped nitrogen from the air. They used this nitrogen to grow tissues.

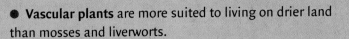
Vascular plants

- **Vascular plants** are more suited to living on drier land than mosses and liverworts.

- **They have branching stems** with tubelike walls that carry water and nutrients.

- **These stems and walls** also mean the plants can stand tall. Vascular plants have spores (reproductive cells, like seeds) – the taller the plant the more widely it can disperse its spores.

- **One of the first known** vascular plants was *Cooksonia*. It was about 5 cm tall, with a forked stem.

- **Scientists called palaeontologists** discovered fossil remains of Cooksonia in Wales. Palaeontologists study fossils of prehistoric plants and animals to see how they lived and evolved.

- **One site where lots** of vascular plant fossils have been found is Rhynie in Scotland.

- **The plants at Rhynie** would have grown on the edges of pools in the Early Devonian Period (about 400 mya).

- **One plant fossil found** at Rhynie is *Aglaophyton*, which stood around 45 cm high.

- *Aglaophyton* had roots and tissues that supported the stem. It also had water-carrying tubes and stomata (tiny openings) that allowed air and water to pass through.

- **Land plants** were essential in providing conditions for animals to make the transition from sea to land. They created soil, food and cover for shelter.

◀ The Cooksonia plant had forked stems ending in spore-filled caps. The earliest examples of Cooksonia have been found in Ireland, dating to around 430 mya.

Ferns

- **Ferns are flowerless**, spore-producing plants, with roots, stems, and leaves called fronds.

- **They developed from** the earliest vascular plants, such as *Cooksonia*.

- **Ferns first appeared** in the Devonian Period (410–355 mya).

- *Cladoxylon* was an early, primitive fern. It had a main stem, forked branches and leaves, and fan-shaped structures that contained spores.

- **During the Carboniferous Period** (355–298 mya), ferns became some of the most abundant plants on Earth.

▼ The underside of a fern frond (leaf), dotted with spore cases. Some types of ferns look exactly the same now as they did more than 200 mya.

> ★ STAR FACT ★
> Ferns remain successful plants today – there are over 12,000 living varieties.

- **Prehistoric ferns** would have looked similar to modern ones, but they could grow much larger. Large ferns are called tree-ferns.

- **Sometimes palaeontologists** find many fossilized fern spores in a single layer of rock. These 'fern spikes' show that there were a lot of ferns around at a particular time.

- **There is a major fern spike** from rock layers that are around 65 million years old, when many other plants had died out, along with dinosaurs and other animals. This fern spike shows that ferns were not affected by the extinctions.

- **Ferns are great survivors** – after volcanic eruptions, they are the first plants to grow again in a landscape.

Clubmosses

● **Clubmosses are covered** with tiny spiral-patterned leaves. Near the top of the stem are club-shaped structures that produce spores.

● **Clubmosses started to grow** in the Devonian Period (410–355 mya).

● **Early clubmosses** included *Baragwanathia* and *Sawdonia*.

● **Another early clubmoss** was *Asteroxylon*. It had forked branches with tiny leaves called leaflets.

● **By the Late Devonian Period**, clubmosses evolved into bigger forms and produced the first tree-sized plants, such as *Lepidodendron*.

● **Lepidodendron trees** could grow more than 30 m high. The diameter of their trunks could be over 2 m.

● **Lepidodendron grew** all over the world in the Carboniferous Period (355–298 mya).

● **It produced large spores** inside cone-shaped containers.

● **Some clubmosses** survive to this day, including *Lycopodium*.

◀ Fossilized Lepidodendron bark shows that the trunks of these giant clubmosses were covered in diamond-shaped patterns. Lepidodendron leaves could be up to 1 m long, and its roots stretched out for up to 12 m.

Gymnosperms

● **Gymnosperms** are plants that produce exposed seeds on the surface of structures such as cones. The word gymnosperm comes from two Greek words: *gymnos*, meaning 'naked', and *sperma*, meaning 'seed'.

● **They first appeared** about 370 mya. Like ferns, they probably developed from early plants such as *Cooksonia*.

● **Gymnosperms grew well** in the damp, tropical forests of the Carboniferous Period (355–298 mya).

● **Varieties of gymnosperm** include conifers, cycads and seed-ferns.

● **Cycads** are plants with feathery tops. They were more common in prehistoric times than today.

▶ These modern pine cones each surround many individual seeds. When the seeds are ripe, the cones open so that the seeds can fall out. Early gymnosperms had less sophisticated seed containers, which consisted of forked branches that loosely held the seeds in place.

● **One type of cycad** is the maidenhair tree, *Gingko biloba*. It still grows in towns and cities, but is now very rare in the wild.

● **One extinct gymnosperm** is *Glossopteris*, which some palaeontologists believe is the ancestor of later flowering plants.

● **Together with ferns and horsetails** (a type of herb), gymnosperms dominated landscapes during the Mesozoic Era (250–65 mya).

● **In the Jurassic Period** (208–144 mya), plant-eating dinosaurs ate their way through huge areas of coniferous forest.

● **In response**, conifers developed tough leaves, sharp needles and poisons.

Angiosperms

- **Angiosperms** are flowering plants. They produce seeds within an ovary, which is contained within a flower. The word comes from the Greek terms *angeion*, meaning 'vessel', and *sperma*, meaning 'seed'.

- **Angiosperms** first appeared about 140 mya.

- **The earliest evidence** of flowering plants comes from the fossil remains of leaves and pollen grains.

- **Plant experts** used to think that magnolias were one of the first angiosperms, but now they think that an extinct plant called *Archaefructus* was older. It lived about 145 mya.

- **Fossil remains** of *Archaefructus* were discovered in northeast China in the mid to late 1990s.

▶ *An Archaefructus plant, which some scientists think is the earliest-known example of an angiosperm. The Archaefructus fossil, which may be around 145 million years old, has a number of angiosperm features including enclosed seeds and flowers.*

- **By 100 mya**, angiosperms had developed into dozens of families of flowering plants, most of which still survive.

- **By 60 mya**, angiosperms had taken over from gymnosperms as the dominant plants on Earth.

- **The start of the Tertiary Period** (65 mya) saw a rise in temperatures that produced the right conditions for tropical rainforests.

- **It was in the rainforests** that angiosperms evolved into many, many different types of plants.

- **Angiosperms** were so successful as they grew quickly, they had extensive roots to anchor them and take up water and nutrients, and they could grow in a wide range of environments .

Forests

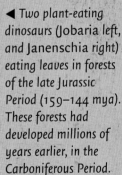

- **The Carboniferous Period** (355–298 mya) was the time of the greatest forests on Earth.

- **The damp climate** of this period suited forests, as did the huge number of swamps in which many trees grew.

◀ *Two plant-eating dinosaurs (Jobaria left, and Janenschia right) eating leaves in forests of the late Jurassic Period (159–144 mya). These forests had developed millions of years earlier, in the Carboniferous Period.*

- **Carboniferous forests** contained huge clubmosses, growing up to 50 m tall, as well as tree-ferns and primitive conifers, such as *Archaeopteris*.

- **The huge numbers of enormous trees** in this period produced the highest levels of oxygen there has ever been on Earth.

- **Dead forest trees** fell and formed mats of rotting wood, which over time turned into peat.

- **Layers of sandstone or other rock** formed over the peat. The pressure of these new layers eventually caused the peat to dry and harden into coal.

- **Coal deposits** are rich sources of fossilized animals.

- **In later periods**, following the Carboniferous Period, plant-eating dinosaurs ate huge areas of forest.

- **Forests were home** to many prehistoric animals, including the first mammals, such as *Megazostrodon* and *Morganucodon*, which hid from predators amongst the trees.

- **By the Tertiary Period** (65–1.6 mya), forests contained many more deciduous (leaf-shedding) trees, such as magnolias, than evergreens, such as conifers.

Grasslands

▶ Etosha National Park, Namibia, South Africa. Grasses did not appear on Earth until around 50 mya. Their ability to withstand drought, fire and grazing are part of the reason why they spread so successfully across the world.

● **In the Oligocene Epoch** (37–24 mya), the Earth's climate became cooler, causing the ice cap covering Antarctica to increase in size.

● **As a result**, tropical rainforests began to decline and grasslands became increasingly common.

● **Grasslands** are called many things in different parts of the world: plains, savannahs, steppes, veldt and prairies.

● **The change from one ecosystem** to another, such as forest to grassland, is called succession. It is a continual process and in central Australia, for example, prehistoric grasslands have been succeeded by desert.

● **Grasses provided** an abundant source of food.

● **Grasses can be cropped** without destroying the plant itself, so they provide animals with a constant supply of food.

● **Grasses are tougher** than forest plants. This meant that plant eaters had to develop strong teeth and better digestive systems.

● **The open nature of grasslands** meant that mammals had to become faster runners, too – to chase after prey or to escape predators.

● **About 11,000 years ago** temperatures began to rise and many grasslands dried out. Lush, mixed grasses gave way to much coarser grasses and scrub – or to desert.

● **This change led** to the extinction of many prehistoric herbivores, such as camel and horse species.

The first invertebrates

● **An invertebrate** is an animal that does not have a spinal column. Invertebrates were the first animals to live on Earth, in the seas.

● **The first animal-like** organisms that fed on other organisms or organic matter were single-celled and sometimes called protozoans.

● **Only prehistoric protozoans** with hard parts survive as fossils. The earliest fossils are around 700 million years old.

● **One of the earliest fossils** of a multi-celled animal is around 600 million years old. This is a creature called *Mawsonites*, which may have been a jellyfish or worm.

◀ Charnia *was a prehistoric animal that grew in feather-like colonies attached to the seabed, like living sea pens.*

● **Most of the earliest** invertebrate fossils are from extinct groups of animals.

● **Some of these animals** had segmented bodies that looked a bit like quilts.

● **One such invertebrate** is *Spriggina*, which is named after Reg Sprigg, a geologist. He discovered its fossilized remains near Ediacara in southern Australia in 1946.

● **Palaeontologists have unearthed** the fossils of many other jellyfish-like invertebrates from Ediacara.

● **Another famous invertebrate** discovery was made by Roger Mason, an English schoolboy, in 1957. This was the fossil of *Charnia*, an animal similar to a living sea pen.

★ STAR FACT ★

Spriggina has a curved, shieldlike end to one part of its body. Some palaeontologists think this was its head, while others think it was an anchor that secured it to the sea bed.

More early invertebrates

● **The early, quilted invertebrates** were extinct by the beginning of the Cambrian Period (542–490 mya).

● **Palaeontologists** regard their extinction as a loss that compares with the death of the dinosaurs at the end of the Cretaceous Period (around 65 mya).

● **Small, shelled invertebrates** emerged in the Early Cambrian Period.

● **These creatures included** the archaeocyathids, which had bodies that were like two cups, one inside the other.

● **Living animals** that most closely resemble archaeocyathids are sponges and corals.

● **Other small**, shelled invertebrates included animals such as *Tommotia* and *Latouchella*. They may have been early molluscs, the ancestors of snails and clams.

● **Tommotia and Latouchella** left behind fossils of their shells, which have strange-looking horns and tubes on the surface.

● **Other Early Cambrian invertebrates**, such as wormlike creatures, did not live in shells. Once predators began to appear, they would have made easy pickings.

● **Invertebrates therefore evolved** defences against hunters, such as a tough exoskeleton (outer skeleton).

● **Another defence was hiding**. Many invertebrates, from worms to arthropods, began to burrow into the sea floor.

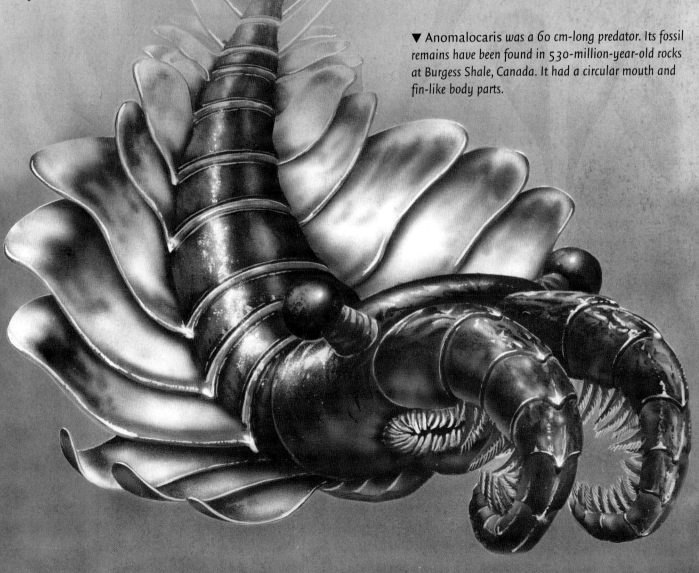

▼ Anomalocaris was a 60 cm-long predator. Its fossil remains have been found in 530-million-year-old rocks at Burgess Shale, Canada. It had a circular mouth and fin-like body parts.

Molluscs and graptolites

- **Modern molluscs** include gastropods (slugs, snails and limpets), bivalves (clams, oysters, mussels and cockles) and cephalopods (octopuses, squids and cuttlefish).

- **Modern and prehistoric molluscs** represent one of the most diverse animal groups ever to have lived.

- **The first molluscs were tiny** – the size of a pinhead. They appeared in Cambrian Period, about 542 mya.

- **The first cephalopod molluscs** emerged towards the end of the Cambrian Period, around 490 mya.

- **One early cephalod** was *Plectronoceras*, which had a horn-shaped shell divided into different chambers.

- **Graptolites** had tentacles that they used to sieve food particles from water or the seabed.

- **Gastropod molluscs** (snails and slugs) were one of the first groups of animals to live on land.

- **Snails and slugs** are limited to where they can live on land as they require moist conditions.

▶ This snail is a mollusc. It has a muscular foot, a head with eyes and tentacles and a shell. Today there are more than 100,000 species of molluscs but many more times this number lived in the past. Their shells make good fossils, and some types evolved quickly, so their changing shapes are used as 'marker fossils' to date rocks.

- **Cephalopods** are the most highly developed of all molluscs. Squids and octopuses evolved big brains, good eyesight, tentacles and beaklike jaws.

- **Graptolites** are an extinct group of molluscs that lived in string-like communities, like lines. Graptolite means 'written stone' because the fossils of the lines of these creatures resemble scrawled handwriting.

Ammonites

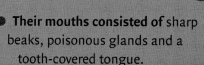

▶ A rock containing an ammonite fossil, displaying the shell's different chambers. The innermost chamber was the home of a newborn ammonite. As it grew, it built a bigger chamber and moved into it.

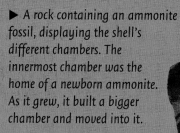

- **Ammonites** belong to the cephalopod group of molluscs.

- **They were once widespread** in the oceans, but, like the dinosaurs, died out at the end of the Cretaceous Period (about 65 mya).

- **The number of ammonite fossils** that have been found proves how plentiful these animals once were.

- **Ammonites were predators** and scavengers. They had good vision, long seizing tentacles and powerful mouths.

- **Their mouths consisted of** sharp beaks, poisonous glands and a tooth-covered tongue.

- **Ammonites had** multi-chambered shells that contained gas and worked like flotation tanks, keeping the creatures afloat.

- *Stephanoceras* was an ammonite with a spiral, disc-shaped shell, 20 cm across. It was very common in the seas of the Mesozoic Era (250–65 mya).

- **The closest living relative** of ammonites is the nautilus, a cephalopod that lives near the seabed.

- **People once thought** that ammonite fossils were the fossils of curled-up snakes.

- **Builders have traditionally set** ammonite fossils into the walls of buildings for decoration.

Worms

- **Worms** are invertebrates that usually have long, soft, slender bodies.

- **They were among the earliest** multi-celled animals to live in the prehistoric seas.

- **The soft bodies of worms** means that they do not make good fossils.

- **Much of our knowledge** of prehistoric worms comes from trace fossils, which include tracks, tunnels and the impressions of their bodies in fine-grained rocks.

- **The tracks and trails** of early worms show that they were mobile creatures, which probably grazed the microbes that covered the sea floor.

- **The 530 million-year-old** mudstone deposits of the Burgess Shale, Canada contain fossil impressions of worms.

- **Some of the Burgess Shale worms** like *Canadia* and *Burgessochaeta*, had thousands of hairlike bristles.

- **Canadia** is an annelid worm. The body is divided into segments. It is thought that millipedes and other arthropods evolved from annelids.

- **Some types of worms,** such as serpulid worms, secrete tubes, which they live in and which contain durable minerals.

- **Remains of serpulids' tubes** are common in rocks of the Mesozoic and Cenozoic Eras (250 mya to the present).

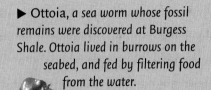

▶ Ottoia, *a sea worm whose fossil remains were discovered at Burgess Shale. Ottoia lived in burrows on the seabed, and fed by filtering food from the water.*

Trilobites

- **Trilobites** belonged to the invertebrate group called arthropods – animals with segmented bodies and hard outer skeletons.

- **Trilobite means** 'three lobes'. Trilobites' hard outer shells were divided into three parts.

- **The first trilobites** appeared about 530 mya. By 500 mya, they had developed into many different types.

- **Trilobites had compound eyes**, like insects' eyes, which could see in many different directions at once.

- **Some trilobites** could roll up into a ball, like some woodlice do today. This was a useful means of protection.

- **Trilobites had long**, thin, jointed legs. They moved quickly over the seabed or sediment covering it.

- **Trilobites moulted** by shedding their outer skeletons. Most trilobite fossils are the remains of shed skeletons.

- **One of the largest trilobites** was *Isotelus*, which grew up to 44 cm long.

- **Trilobites could also be** much smaller, such as *Conocoryphe*, which was about 2 cm long.

- **Trilobites became extinct** around 250 mya – along with huge numbers of other marine animals.

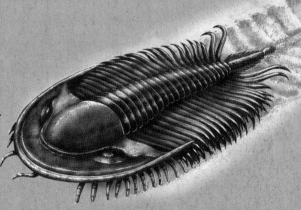

▲ Conocoryphe *trilobites lived in the seas of the Mid-Cambrian Period, about 530 mya. It was one of the smaller trilobites.*

Pterygotus

- **Pterygotus** was an enormous water scorpion that grew up to 2.3 m long.

- **Fossils of Pterygotus** have been found in rocks of the Silurian Period (435–410 mya).

- **Pterygotus** was a fearsome hunter, equipped with large eyes and long claws.

- **It had two huge claws** (called chelicerae) for grasping prey, two paddles for swimming, and eight legs for chasing victims over the seabed and digging them up from the sediment.

- **Pterygotus belonged** to the group of invertebrates known as eurypterids (water scorpions).

- **Eurypterids** lived between 490 and 250 mya.

- **Not all eurypterids were giants** – some were only 10 cm long.

★ STAR FACT ★
Dolphins swim by beating their tails up and down – which is how palaeontologists think *Pterygotus* swam.

- **They were not true scorpions**, because their tail parts (called the opisthosoma) served as swimming paddles, not stinging weapons.

- **Pterygotus' opisthosoma** was long and ended in a flattened paddle. Palaeontologists think it swam by beating this paddle up and down.

▼ Pterygotus, which was bigger than a human, was the largest arthropod (an animal with a segmented body and a hard outer skeleton) ever to have lived.

Insects, centipedes and millipedes

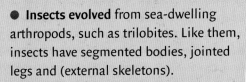

- **Insects evolved** from sea-dwelling arthropods, such as trilobites. Like them, insects have segmented bodies, jointed legs and (external skeletons).

- **The first land-living insects** appeared in the Devonian Period (410–355 mya).

- **Insects made the transition** to breathing air on land by developing small tubes called tracheae in their bodies.

- *Rhyniella* was the first known land insect. It was a springtail – an insect still alive today, which eats rotting plants and flips itself into the air if disturbed.

- *Latzelia* was an early centipede that lived on forest floors in the Carboniferous Period (355–298 mya).

- *Latzelia* **had poisonous fangs**, which it used to kill worms and other insects.

◀ The evolution of winged, pollinating insects such as these honey bees is linked to the evolution of flowering plants. Bees, as well as other flying insects, help these plants to spread by carrying pollen from the male part of one flower to the female part of another as they feed off nectar.

- **Insects were the first animals** to achieve flight. Early flying insects had stiff wings, which stuck out from their bodies – similar to dragonflies' wings.

- **The Cretaceous Period** (144–65 mya) saw a big rise in the number of flying insects, because of the emergence of flowering plants.

- **Many flowering plants** rely on flying insects to spread their pollen, while flying insects, such as bees, rely on flowers for food (nectar and pollen).

- **Beelike insects** date back to the Late Cretaceous Period, while modern bees first appeared around 30 mya.

Monster mini-beasts

- **The biggest insects** ever known lived in the forests of the Carboniferous Period (355–298 mya).

- **The size of flying insects** increased with the size of trees. One explanation for this is that they needed to fly higher to feed on the insects that lived in the tall trees.

- *Meganeura* was the biggest winged insect, with a wingspan of 70 cm. It was 15 times the size of a dragonfly.

- **Like modern dragonflies**, *Meganeura* was unable to fold back its wings when it was resting.

- **The Carboniferous forests** were also home to enormous millipedes. They are known to palaeontologists because of fossilized traces of their footprints. Some of these millipedes might have been as long as a human is tall.

- **Some millipedes** had poisonous fangs. A human-sized, poisonous millipede must have been a terrifying predator.

- **Mega-insects did not live** only in the Carboniferous Period. *Formicium giganteum* was a giant ant that lived about 45 mya.

▶ Like this modern-day dragonfly, Meganeura had large eyes that allowed it to spot the movements of potential prey.

- **Worker giant ants** grew up to 3 cm long, but queens were nearly 6 cm, with a wingspan of 13 cm – bigger than some small birds!

- *Formicium giganteum's* closest living relative is the red wood ant.

★ STAR FACT ★
Another huge Carboniferous dragonfly is known as the 'Bolsover dragonfly', since its remains were discovered in Bolsover, England. It was the size of a seagull.

Pikaia

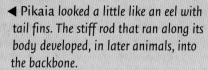

- **Pikaia** was a small, wormlike creature that is thought to be the ancestor of all backboned animals.

- **Its fossil remains** were found in the 530 million-year-old mudstone deposits of the Burgess Shale in Canada.

- **Pikaia** was the first-known chordate, an animal with a supporting rod, called a notochord, along its back. All vertebrates belong to this group, as well as marine animals called tunicates and acraniates.

- **Pikaia was 5 cm long** with a notochord (stiffening rod) running along its body – a kind of primitive spine that gave its body flexibility.

- **The notochord** allowed the animal's muscles to work against it, and the animal's body organs to hang from it.

- **Pikaia is similar** to a modern creature called *Branchiostoma*, a small, transparent creature that lives in sand on the seabed.

◀ *Pikaia looked a little like an eel with tail fins. The stiff rod that ran along its body developed, in later animals, into the backbone.*

- **As it lacked a bony skeleton**, a backbone, ribs, paired fins and jaws, *Pikaia* was not really a fish.

- **Pikaia was a more complex creature** than many other animals found in the Burgess Shale. It suggests that other complex creatures must have lived before it, although there is no fossil evidence for this.

- **The head of the** *Pikaia* was very primitive, with a pair of tentacles, a mouth and a simple brain (a swelling of the nerve cord) for processing information.

- **Pikaia swam** in a zig-zag fashion, similar to sea snakes.

Jawless fish

- **The first fish appeared** in the Late Cambrian Period, about 500 mya.

- **These fish had permanently** gaping mouths – as they had no jaws they could not open and close their mouths.

- **Early fish were called** agnathans, which means 'jawless'.

- **Agnathans ate by** sieving plankton through their simple mouth opening, as well as scooping up algae on the seabed.

★ **STAR FACT** ★
Hemicyclaspis had eyes on top of its head. This suggests it lived on the seabed, and used its eyes to keep a lookout for predators above.

- **Among the oldest** complete agnathan fossils are *Arandaspis*, which comes from Australia, and *Sacabambaspis*, which comes from Bolivia.

- *Hemicyclaspis* was another agnathan. It was a very flat fish, with a broad head shield and a long tail.

- **Later jawless fish** had more streamlined, deeper bodies and eyes at the front of their heads. This suggests they were not restricted to the seabed.

- **Most jawless fish** died out by the end of the Devonian Period (around 350 mya).

- **Living relatives of agnathans** include lampreys and hagfish, which have soft bodies and look like eels. Like agnathans, they are also jawless.

▲ *Early jawless fish such as Hemicyclaspis, could swim much farther and quicker than most invertebrates. This meant they could more easily search for and move to new feeding areas.*

Jawed fish

● **The first jawed fish** emerged in the Early Silurian Period (about 430 mya).

● **Palaeontologists** call jawed fish acanthodians, from the Greek word *akantha*, meaning 'thorn' or 'spine'.

● **Jaws and teeth** meant acanthodians could eat a greater variety of food and defend themselves more effectively.

● **Jaws and teeth allowed** acanthodians to become predators.

● **Acanthodians' jaws** evolved from gill arches in the pharynx, the tube that runs from the mouth to the stomach.

● **Gill arches** are bony rods and muscles that surround the gills, the breathing organs of a fish.

● **As acanthodians developed jaws**, they developed teeth, too.

● **The earliest fish teeth** were conelike shapes along the jaw, made out of bone and coated with hard enamel.

● **The teeth of early acanthodians** varied. In some species they were sharp and spiky, in others they were like blades while in others they resembled flat plates.

◀ Climatius, *a type of acanthodian or jawed fish, that lived around 400 mya. Another name for acanthodians is 'spiny sharks' – although they were not sharks, many had spines on the edges of their fins.*

Placoderms

● **Placoderms** were jawed fish that had bony plates covering the front part of the body.

● **They appeared** in the Late Silurian Period (415 mya) and were abundant in the seas of the Devonian Period (410–355 mya).

● **Placoderm means 'plated skin'.** The plating provided protection against predators.

● **Most placoderms** ranged in length from 30 cm to 10 m.

● **The two groups** of placoderms were arthrodires and antiarchs.

● **Arthrodires** could turn their head in many directions.

● **Arthrodires had powerful jaws** and sharp teeth.

● **Antiarchs were smaller** than arthrodires. Like arthrodires, the head and front part of its body were covered in bony plates.

▲ Bothriolepis *had eyes on top of its head. Its mouth was lined by cutting plates situated under the head. This lead palaeontologists to believe that it was a bottom-dwelling feeder.*

● **Antiarchs also had a pectoral** (front end) fin connected to its head plates. Palaeontologists think they might have used this fin as a leg, to help it move over the seabed.

Sharks

◀ Hybodus *was a blunt-headed prehistoric shark that lived between 250 and 125 mya, in the time of the dinosaurs. It looked quite similar to modern sharks, but had different jaws.*

● **The earliest-known** shark fossils come from rock layers of the Early Devonian Period (410–355 mya).

● **Sharks belong to the group** known as cartilaginous fish, which also includes rays and skates. Their skeletons are made from cartilage, not bone.

● *Cladoselache* was a prehistoric shark, which could grow up to 2 m long.

● *Cladoselache* **appears to have been** quite similar to a modern shark – it had a streamlined body, a pair of dorsal (back) fins and triangular-shaped pectoral (front end) fins.

● **Early sharks hunted squid,** small fish and crustaceans.

● *Stethacanthus* **was a prehistoric shark** that looked nothing like a modern one. It had an anvil-shaped projection above its head, which was covered in teeth.

● *Stethacanthus* **lived** during the Carboniferous Period (355–298 mya).

● **Sharks are at the top of the food chain** in modern seas, but this was not the case during the Devonian Period.

● **Placoderms,** such as *Dunkleosteus,* dwarfed even the biggest sharks.

▲ *This modern blue shark, is a fast swimmer and a fierce hunter. The main features of sharks – from their tightly packed, needle-sharp teeth to their streamlined shape – have changed little over 400 million years.*

★ **STAR FACT** ★
Prehistoric sharks' jaws were fixed to the side of their skull, while modern sharks' jaws hang beneath their braincase, which gives them a more powerful bite.

Bony fish

- **Bony fish** have internal skeletons and external scales made of bone.

- **They first appeared** in the Late Devonian Period (around 360 mya).

- **Bony fish evolved** into the most abundant and varied fish in the seas.

- **There are two types** of bony fish – ray-finned fish and lobe-finned fish.

- **There were plenty of** prehistoric lobe-finned fish, but only a few species survive today. They belong to one of two groups – lungfish or coelacanths.

- **Amphibians** – and, ultimately, reptiles and mammals – evolved from lobe-finned fish.

▶ *This modern-day coelacanth is a direct descendant of the lobe-finned bony fish that lived 350 mya. Coelacanths were thought to be extinct until a fisherman caught one off the coast of South Africa in 1938.*

- **Ray-finned fish** were so-called because of the bony rays that supported their fins. Most early ray-finned fish were small, ranging in size from about 5 cm to 20 cm long.

- **Rhadinichthys and Cheirolepis** were two early ray-finned fish. They were small predators, equipped with good swimming ability and snapping jaws.

- **Around 250 mya,** ray-finned fish lost many of the bony rays from their fins. The fins became less stiff and more flexible – and the fish became better swimmers.

- **New types of** ray-finned fish, called teleosts, also developed more symmetrical tails and thinner scales.

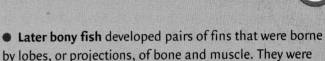

Fins

- **The earliest fish** did not have fins. The first fish to have them were acanthodians (jawed fish).

- **Acanthodians** were the first fish predators. Fins gave them manoeuvrability – needed for chasing their prey.

- **Fins let fish** make quick or subtle changes in direction.

- **They also help fish** to stay afloat and counter gravity, since their bones and muscles are denser than water.

- **This explains why** most agnathans (jawless fish), which lacked fins, lived on the bottom of seas – it meant they did not have to struggle against gravity.

- **Pectoral fins**, at the front end of a fish, help to keep it level and counteract its tendency to pitch forward at the front because of the weight of the head.

- **Dorsal fins**, on a fish's back, and pelvic and anal fins at its rear, stop it from rolling over.

- **The first acanthodians** to have fins had a pair of dorsal fins, a single anal fin beneath the tail and a varying number of pairs of fins on their undersides.

- **Later bony fish** developed pairs of fins that were borne by lobes, or projections, of bone and muscle. They were called lobe-finned fish.

- **The fins of lobe-finned fish** evolved into the limbs of amphibians.

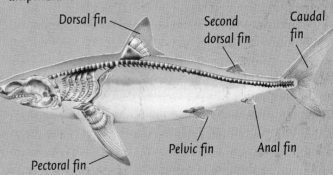

Dorsal fin — Second dorsal fin — Caudal fin — Pectoral fin — Pelvic fin — Anal fin

▲ *The skeleton of a great white shark. On its back is a large dorsal fin followed by a much smaller one. On its front are pairs of pectoral and pelvic fins. The caudal fin, the shark's tail, is used for propulsion and steering.*

From fins to limbs

- **The first land animals with** backbones were tetrapods. They had legs to move around in search of food.

- **Tetrapods** evolved from lobe-finned fish.

- **Fossil skeletons** of the lobe-finned fish *Eusthenopteron* show that the organization of bones in its front and rear fins was similar to the arrangement of limbs in tetrapods.

- *Eusthenopteron* used its fins as legs to move over land.

- **The lobe-finned fish** *Panderichthys*, could more effectively use fins as limbs than *Eusthenopteron*. *Panderichthys* more tetrapod than fish.

★ STAR FACT ★
Suitable fins were not the only feature that meant lobe-finned fish could evolve into land-dwelling animals. They also had lungs for breathing air!

- **The front fins** in lobe-finned fish connected to a shoulder girdle, while the rear fins connected to a hip girdle. These girdles connected to the backbone.

- **These hip and shoulder connections** meant that limbs of future tetrapods were connected to a skeleton, which stopped the limbs pressing on the inside of the body .

- **Tetrapods** developed heads that were separated from their shoulders and joined instead by a neck.

- **Necks** allowed animals to bend down to feed, reach up for food, and turn around to see.

◄ *Eusthenopteron used its fins to move out of the water. Its name means 'good strong fin.'*

Tetrapods

▶ *Eogyrinus was an amphibious tetrapod that lived around 310 mya. It grew up to 4.5 m long and had a skull similar to a crocodile's and a body similar to an eel's.*

- **Tetrapod means** 'four-legged'. Early tetrapods were amphibians – animals that lived in water and on land.

- **The first tetrapods** emerged in the Late Devonian Period (about 360 mya).

- **They lived in shallow freshwater lakes** and rivers. They developed limbs and lungs to cope with the waters drying out and this enabled them to move to new habitats.

- **The size of tetrapods** increased during the Carboniferous Period (355–298 mya). This may have been because there was more oxygen in the atmosphere, produced by the huge Carboniferous forests.

- **Tetrapods adapting to the land** had to face a range of challenges such as greater temperature variations than in water, and more ultraviolet radiation from the Sun.

- **The early tetrapods** were called labyrinthodonts, because of their labyrinth-like tooth structure. These animals include *Ichthyostega*, *Eogyrinus* and *Diadectes*.

- *Diadectes* is the earliest plant-eating vertebrate known. At 3 m long it had small jaws with blunt teeth.

- **Modern amphibians** can be less than 10 cm long, while early tetrapods could grow up to 2 m.

- **Like their living relatives**, frogs, early tetrapods laid eggs in water that hatched into tadpoles.

★ STAR FACT ★
Some early tetrapods had seven digits (fingers and toes). Others had six or even eight. Eventually all tetrapods evolved to have five digits.

Breathing air

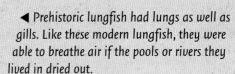

- **Fish breathe oxygen** in water through their gills. When a fish is out of the water, these gills collapse.

- **For creatures to adapt** to living on land, they had to develop air-breathing lungs.

- **Tetrapods** were not the first creatures to develop lungs – this step was taken by lobe-finned fish.

- **Lungfish** are lobe-fins that still exist today. They live in hot places and, when rivers dry out, bury themselves in mud and breathe through lungs.

- **Early tetrapods**, such as *Ichthyostega* and *Acanthostega*, had gills and lungs, which suggests they could breathe in both air and water.

- **Later tetrapods breathed through gills** when they were first born, but, like modern frogs and newts, their gills shrank when they got older and were replaced by lungs.

◀ Prehistoric lungfish had lungs as well as gills. Like these modern lungfish, they were able to breathe air if the pools or rivers they lived in dried out.

- **Modern amphibians** also take in oxygen through their skin, which is soft and moist.

- **Early tetrapods had tougher skin**, so were unable to breathe through it.

- **Breathing through skin** limits an animal's size, which is why modern amphibians are much smaller than many of their prehistoric ancestors.

> **★ STAR FACT ★**
> Animals could only evolve to live on land because of the work of plants over millions of years, producing oxygen that became part of Earth's atmosphere.

Acanthostega

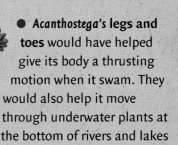

▶ *Acanthostega* may have evolved from lobe-finned fish. It had a number of fishlike features such as gills and lungs, as well as tail fin.

- *Acanthostega* was one of the earliest tetrapods. It had a fishlike body, which suggests it spent most of its life in water.

- **Its fossil remains** were found in rock strata dating from the Late Devonian Period (around 370 mya).

- *Acanthostega's* **body** was about 1 m long.

- **It had a wide tail**, which would have been useful for swimming but inconvenient for moving on land.

- **Its legs were well-developed**, however, with eight toes on the front feet and seven on the rear ones.

- **The number of toes** on its feet surprised palaeontologists – they had previously thought all tetrapods had five toes.

- *Acanthostega's* **legs and toes** would have helped give its body a thrusting motion when it swam. They would also help it move through underwater plants at the bottom of rivers and lakes in search of prey.

- *Acanthostega* had a flattened skull, and its eye sockets were placed close together on the top of its head.

- **A complete but jumbled-up** *Acanthostega* **fossil** was discovered in hard rock in Greenland. Palaeontologists had to work very carefully to prise the fossil from the rock.

> **★ STAR FACT ★**
> *Acanthostega* had fishlike gills for breathing water as well as lungs for breathing air.

Ichthyostega

● **Ichthyostega** was another early tetrapod. Like *Acanthostega*, it was discovered in Greenland in rock that was 370 million years old.

● **Its body was around 1 m long.** Palaeontologists think it was probably covered in scales.

● **Ichthyostega had a flat head,** a long snout, large jaws and teeth.

● **Its body was barrel shaped.** It had short, strong legs and a fishlike tail.

● **This tetrapod ate small fish** and shellfish, but would have been prey for large fish.

● **Ichthyostega had a skull** that was completely solid apart from its eye sockets. This meant that there were no holes around which jaw muscles could attach.

● **Without proper jaw muscles,** *Ichthyostega* and other early tetrapods could do little more than snap their jaws open and shut.

● **Like *Acanthostega*,** *Ichthyostega* was more suited to swimming than walking. It used its legs for paddles, and its tail for manoeuvrability.

● **Ichthyostega also used its limbs** and feet for holding onto plants and digging for shellfish.

● **Ichthyostega and *Acanthostega*** show how animals were slowly adapting from a life in water to one on land.

▼ Scientists think that Ichthyostega's shape and behaviour were similar to that of seals. Like seals, it could probably tuck its limbs alongside its body when swimming. On land, it might have used its forelimbs to drag the rest of its body over the ground.

Temnospondyls

◀ Gerrothorax *was an aquatic temnospondyl of the Late Triassic Period (215–208 mya). Like most other temnospondyls, it was a predator.*

● **Other temnospondyls,** such as *Paracyclotosaurus* and *Cyclotosaurus,* had rounder bodies and thinner heads with powerful teeth and jaws.

● *Gerrothorax, Paracyclotosaurus* and *Cyclotosaurus* were suited to water habitats. Other temnospondyls show more adaptations for land.

● **One temnospondyl** that had a land-adapted body was the sturdily built *Cacops,* which grew to about 40 cm long.

● **A much bigger land-living** temnospondyl was *Eryops,* which grew to about 2 m in length.

● **Temnospondyls** were the most successful land predators of their day.

● **They were all destined for extinction,** however. Temnospondyls were not the ancestors of reptiles – this role belonged to smaller tetrapods.

● **Temnospondyls** were a group of tetrapods that emerged in the Carboniferous Period (355–298 mya). They were some of the biggest early tetrapods.

● *Gerrothorax* was a temnospondyl. It grew up to 1 m or more long and had a flattened body shape and a very wide, flat head, with eyes on top.

● *Gerrothorax* **looked a little like** an enormous tadpole. It probably spent most of its time in water rather than on land.

● **Its flat body shape** suited a life spent hunting by lying at the bottom of swamps and ambushing passing fish.

Lepospondyls

● **Lepospondyls** were another group of early tetrapods. Like temnospondyls, they first appeared between 350 and 300 mya.

● **Lepospondyls were small animals,** often about the size of modern-day newts (10–15 cm long).

● **Their backbones differed** from temnospondyls' backbones.

● **Lepospondyls also had simpler teeth** and fewer bones in their skulls than temnospondyls.

● *Diplocaulus* was a lepospondyl with strange wing shapes, which looked a bit like a boomerang, protruding from its skull.

▲ *One theory about* Diplocaulus' *strange skull shape is that it was a form of defence, and difficult for any predator to swallow. Another idea is that it helped* Diplocaulus *move through the water, like a hydrofoil.*

● **It lived in the Mid Permian Period** (about 275 mya).

● **One *Diplocaulus* fossil** found in the USA was 0.8 m long.

● *Diplocaulus* **lived in freshwater streams.** Its oddly shaped head probably increased its manoeuvrability in the water, like the rudder on a submarine.

● **Lepospondyls** were controversial creatures. Some palaeontologists argue that they were the ancestors of modern amphibians.

> ★ STAR FACT ★
> At least one lepospondyl, *Ophiderpeton,* reversed the trend of the tetrapods by losing all its legs so that it resembled an eel.

Frogs and salamanders

- **Modern amphibians**, such as frogs, toads, salamanders and newts, belong to the group called the lissamphibians.

- **Lissamphibians** evolved between the Late Carboniferous and Early Triassic Periods (300–240 mya).

- **Triadobatrachus lived** in the Early Triassic Period, in Madagascar and was 10 cm long.

- **Triadobatrachus had a froglike skull.** Compared to earlier amphibians, it had a shortened back, with fewer spinal bones, and a shortened tail.

▶ Triadobatrachus *was the earliest-known frog.*

- **Evolution did not stop** with *Triadobatrachus* – modern frogs have even fewer spinal bones and no tail at all.

- *Triadobatrachus'* **hind legs** were the same size as its front legs. Modern frogs have longer hind legs for hopping.

- *Karaurus* is the first known salamander. It lived in the Late Jurassic Period (around 150 mya) in Kazakhstan. It was 19 cm long, with a broad skull.

- **More modern-looking** frog and salamander fossils have been discovered in Messel, Germany. They date from the Early Eocene Epoch (around 50 mya).

- **Some Messel frog fossils** have their legs bent, as if they were in mid-hop. There are even tadpole fossils.

First reptiles

- **Reptiles evolved** from amphibians during the Carboniferous Period (355–298 mya).

- **Unlike amphibians**, which live near and lay their eggs in water, reptiles are more adapted to life on land.

- **Compared to amphibians**, reptiles had better limbs for walking, a more effective circulatory system for moving blood around their bodies, and bigger brains.

- **They also had more powerful jaw muscles** than amphibians and would have been better predators. Early reptiles ate millipedes, spiders and insects.

- **One of the earliest reptiles** was a small creature called *Hylonomus*, which lived in the Mid Carboniferous Period.

- *Hylonomus* lived in forests on the edges of lakes and rivers. Fossil remains of this reptile have been found inside the stumps of clubmoss trees.

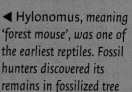

◀ Hylonomus, *meaning 'forest mouse', was one of the earliest reptiles. Fossil hunters discovered its remains in fossilized tree stumps in Nova Scotia, Canada.*

- **Another early reptile** was *Paleothyris*. Like *Hylonomus*, it was about 20 cm long, and had a smaller head than amphibians.

- **One animal that represents** a staging post between amphibians and reptiles is *Westlothiana lizziae*, which was discovered in Scotland in the 1980s.

- *Westlothiana lizziae* lived in the Early Carboniferous Period (about 340 mya).

- **At first palaeontologists thought** that *Westlothiana lizziae* was the oldest reptile. But its backbone, head and legs are closer to those of an amphibian.

Eggs

● **Reptiles' eggs** are a major evolutionary advance over amphibians' eggs.

● **Early amphibians**, like modern ones, laid their eggs in water. This is because their eggs were covered in jelly (like modern frogspawn) and would dry out on land.

● **Reptiles evolved eggs** that were covered by a shell. This meant they could lay them on land and they would not dry out.

● **Shelled eggs** meant that reptiles did not have to return to water to lay them.

● **Another advantage** was that reptiles could hide their eggs on land. Eggs laid in water are easy pickings for hungry animals.

● **Reptiles' embryos** complete their growth phases inside eggs – when they hatch they look like miniature adults.

● **In contrast**, baby amphibians hatch from eggs as larvae, such as tadpoles. They live in water and breathe with gills before they develop lungs and can live on land.

● **Reptile shells are hard**, and protect the growing reptile embryos. They also provide them with food while they develop.

● **During the evolution** from amphibians to reptiles, some tetrapods laid jelly-covered eggs on land.

● **A number of living amphibians** lay jelly-covered eggs on land, including some tropical frogs and mountain salamanders.

◄ *A female snake protecting her eggs. Eggs laid on land are easier to protect than those laid in water.*

Skulls

● **The jaws of reptiles** are another feature that shows the evolutionary progression from amphibians.

● **Amphibians' jaws** are designed to snap but not to bite together tightly.

● **In contrast**, reptiles had more jaw muscles and could press their jaws together firmly. This meant they could break insect body casings and chew tough plant stems.

● **By the Late Carboniferous Period** (about 300 mya), reptiles developed openings in their skulls, behind the eye socket. These allowed room for more jaw muscles.

● **Four types of reptile skull** developed. Each belonged to a different type of reptile.

● **Anapsids had no openings** in their skull other than the eye sockets.

★ **STAR FACT** ★
Plants developed tough stems and leaves, spines and poisons to protect themselves frum hungry reptiles.

● **Euryapsids had one opening** high up on either side of the skull. Sea reptiles, such as ichthyosaurs, were euryapsids, but this group has no surviving relatives.

● **Synapsids** had one opening low down on either side of the skull. Mammals are descended from this group.

● **Diapsids had two openings** on either side of the skull. Dinosaurs and pterosaurs were diapsids; so too are birds and crocodiles.

◄ *Varanosaurus was a synapsid reptile that lived in the Early Permian Period, about 290 mya. There are important similarities between the skulls of synapsid reptiles and mammals.*

Synapsids

- **Synapsids** were a group of reptiles that had a pair of openings on their lower skull, behind the eye socket, to which their jaw were attached.

- **Synapsids are the ancestors** of mammals, which explains why they are sometimes called 'mammal-like reptiles'.

- **These reptiles** first appeared in the Late Carboniferous Period (about 310 mya). They were dominant animals in the Permian and Triassic Periods (298–208 mya).

- **The first synapsids** are called pelycosaurs. They were heavy-bodied and walked a bit like modern-day crocodiles.

- **Dimetrodon** and the *Edaphosaurus* – both of which had long, fanlike spines on their backs – were pelycosaurs.

- **Later synapsids** are called therapsids. The earliest ones had bigger skulls and jaws than pelycosaurs, as well as longer legs and shorter tails.

◄ *Diictodon* was a mammal-like reptile that lived about 260 mya. A plant eater and a burrower, it was an advanced form of a synapsid known as a dicynodont.

- **Later therapsids** are split into subgroups – dicynodonts and cynodonts. Dicynodont means 'two dog teeth' – cynodont means 'dog tooth'.

- **Dicynodonts were herbivores.** Most had rounded bodies and beaks that they used to cut plant stems.

- **Cynodonts were carnivores.** They used different teeth for different tasks – for stabbing, nipping and chewing.

- **Cynodonts were the most mammal-like** of all reptiles. Some had whiskers and may have been warm-blooded.

Dimetrodon

- **Dimetrodon** was an early synapsid reptile called a pelycosaur.

- **It was a carnivore**, and was one of the first land animals that could kill creatures its own size (about 3.5 m long).

- **Dimetrodon had a tall**, skinny fin – a bit like a sail – running along its backbone. This fin was formed by a row of long spines that grew out of separate vertebrae.

- **Blood flowing** inside this sail would have been warmed by the early morning sun and carried to the rest of the body. The sail could also have radiated heat out, preventing overheating.

- **As a result,** *Dimetrodon* would warm up more quickly than other reptiles, so it could hunt them while they were still sluggish, cold or asleep.

- **Dimetrodon had a deep skull** and sharp, dagger-like teeth of different sizes. Its name means 'two shapes of teeth'.

► As well as allowing its body to quickly warm up or cool down, Dimetrodon's large fin might have helped it to attract mates or ward off rivals.

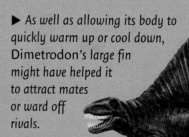

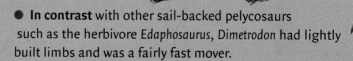

- **In contrast** with other sail-backed pelycosaurs such as the herbivore *Edaphosaurus*, *Dimetrodon* had lightly built limbs and was a fairly fast mover.

- **Dimetrodon was one** of the dominant land predators between 280 and 260 mya.

- **After that time**, however, other reptiles, known as archosaurs, began to eclipse *Dimetrodon* because they were even bigger and better hunters.

- **Dimetrodon was extinct** by the beginning of the Triassic Period (about 250 mya).

Moschops

- **Moschops** was a later synapsid reptile called a therapsid. It belonged to a group of reptiles called dinocephalians (meaning 'terrible heads'), because it had a very big skull.

- **It was a plant eater**, and was probably preyed upon by large flesh-eating dinocephalians, such as *Titanosuchus*.

- **Moschops lived** in the Permian Period (298–250 mya) in southern Africa.

- **It grew up to 5 m long**. It had a squat body and a short tail. Stocky limbs held it well off the ground.

- **Moschops had many** peglike, chisel-edged teeth, which were adapted for biting and uprooting plant matter.

- **Its back sloped downwards** from the front, rather like a giraffe's.

- ◄ The bones on the top of Moschops' skull could be up to 10 cm thick – enough to withstand the blows from head-butting rivals or enemies.

- **It had enormous limb girdles** for both its front and rear legs, to support its heavy weight.

- **Moschops had a high skull** with an extremely thick bone on top, which it may have used to head-butt its rivals or enemies.

- **Its skull bones** became thicker as it got older. This thickening of the skull is called pachyostosis.

- **While Moschops' skull** was very big, its brain was not. 'Bone head' might be a good nickname for it!

Cynognathus

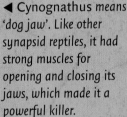

- **Cynognathus** was a therapsid reptile called a cynodont.

- **It lived** in the Early to Mid Triassic Period (250–220 mya).

- **Cynognathus was the size** of a large wolf, and weighed between 40 and 50 kg.

- **Its skull was about 40 cm long**, and its total body length was around 2 m.

- **Like modern wolves**, *Cynognathus* was an active predator.

- **Cynognathus had** some very mammal-like features. Palaeontologists think it may have been warm-blooded, may have had hair on its skin, and may have given birth to live young.

- **One of the many features** *Cynognathus* had in common with mammals was a bony palate that separated the mouth from the nasal cavity, and allowed it to breathe as it ate.

- ◄ Cynognathus means 'dog jaw'. Like other synapsid reptiles, it had strong muscles for opening and closing its jaws, which made it a powerful killer.

- **Its teeth were similar** to a dog's. It had incisors (front teeth) for cutting, canines (teeth next to incisors) for piercing and molars (cheek teeth) for slicing.

- **The legs were designed** for fast running – they were tucked underneath and close to its body unlike the legs of Moschops, which stuck out more at the sides.

- **Fossil skeletons of** *Cynognathus* have been found in South Africa. Palaeontologists think that it favoured hunting in dry, desert-like areas.

Crocodilians

● **The first crocodile-like reptiles** were called eosuchians, meaning 'dawn crocodiles'. They appeared in the Permian Period (298–250 mya).

● **The first true crocodiles** appeared at the end of the Triassic Period (about 215 mya). They were called protosuchians, and lived in pools and rivers.

● *Protosuchus* had a short skull and sharp teeth, and would have looked quite like a modern crocodile.

● **Other early crocodiles,** such as *Terrestrisuchus*, looked less like modern crocodiles.

● *Terrestrisuchus* had a short body and long legs. Its name means 'land crocodile', as it may have been more at home on land than in water.

● **The next group of crocodilians** to evolve were the mesosuchians, which lived in the sea.

● **One subgroup** of mesosuchians, the eusuchians, are the ancestors of modern crocodiles.

● *Metriorhynchus* was a marine mesosuchian. It had flippers instead of limbs, and sharp, fish-stabbing teeth. It lived in the Late Jurassic Period (around 150 mya).

● *Deinosuchus* was an eusuchian. It was thought to be the largest-ever crocodile at 11 m long until a recent discovery of a *Sarchosuchus* fossil estimated to measure 15 m.

▼ Fossils of Protosuchus *have been discovered in Arizona, dating to around 200 mya. Although similar to living crocodiles in many ways, its legs were much longer.*

★ STAR FACT ★
Modern crocodiles are living fossils.
They look similar to the crocodiles that
were alive 100 mya.

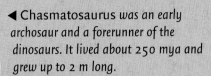

Archosaurs

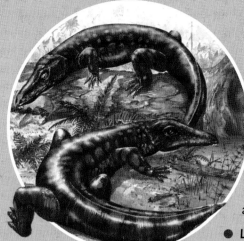

- **The archosaurs** (meaning 'ruling reptiles') dominated land, seas and skies in the Mesozoic Era (250–65 mya).

- **Archosaurs** included crocodilians, dinosaurs and the flying reptiles called pterosaurs.

- **Archosaurs are the ancestors** of modern birds and crocodiles.

- **Archosaurs were diapsid reptiles** – they had two openings in the skull to which jaw muscles were attached, which meant their jaws were very powerful.

- **The first archosaurs** appeared in the Permian Period (around 255 mya). They would have looked like lizards, but with shorter bodies and longer legs and necks.

- **One early archosaur** was *Chasmatosaurus*. It had a large, heavy body, and probably spent most of its time hunting in rivers.

- ◀ Chasmatosaurus *was an early archosaur and a forerunner of the dinosaurs. It lived about 250 mya and grew up to 2 m long.*

- **Lagosuchus** was another early archosaur. Some palaeontologists think it might have been the direct ancestor of the dinosaurs.

- **Lagosuchus was very small.** It was about 30 cm long and weighed about 90 g. It had a slender body, and ran on its hind legs.

- **The name** *Lagosuchus* means 'rabbit crocodile' – palaeontologists think it may have moved by hopping.

> ★ STAR FACT ★
> Like many later dinosaurs, some early archosaurs were bipedal (two-legged walkers), leaving their arms free.

Placodonts

- **After adapting** so well to life on land, some groups of reptiles evolved into water-dwelling creatures.

- **Placodonts were early aquatic** (water-living) reptiles. They lived in the Mid Triassic Period (240–220 mya).

- **The name placodont** means 'plate tooth'. These reptiles had large cheek teeth that worked like large crushing plates.

- **Placodonts appeared** at about the same time as another group of aquatic reptiles, called nothosaurs.

- **They had shorter,** sturdier bodies than the nothosaurs but, like them, did not survive as a group for a very long time.

- *Placodus* **was a placodont.** It had a stocky body, stumpy limbs, and webbed toes for paddling. It may have had a fin on its tail.

- *Placodus* **means 'flat tooth'.** It probably used its flat teeth, which pointed outwards from its mouth, to prise shellfish off rocks.

- *Psephoderma* was a turtle-like placodont. Its body was covered in a shell, which in turn was covered by hard plates.

- *Psephoderma* **also had** a horny beak, like a turtle's, and paddle-shaped limbs.

- *Henodus* was another turtle-like placodont. It also had a beak, which it probably used to grab molluscs from the sea bed.

◀ Placodus *was 2 m long, and probably used its sticking-out front teeth to scrape up molluscs from the seabed. Its platelike side teeth would then make short work of crunching the molluscs.*

Nothosaurs

- **Nothosaurs** were another group of reptiles that returned to live in the seas.

- **Nothosaurus was**, as its name implies, a nothosaur. Its neck, tail and body were all long and flexible.

- **Its total length** was about 3 m and its approximate weight was 200 kg.

- **Impressions left** in some *Nothosaurus* fossils show that it had webs between its toes.

- **Nothosaurus' jaw** had many sharp, interlocking teeth, which would have crunched up the fish and shrimps on which it fed.

- **Ceresiosaurus** was another nothosaur. Palaeontologists think it swam by swaying its body and tail from side to side, like a fish.

- **Ceresiosaurus means** 'deadly lizard'. It was bigger than *Nothosaurus* at 4 m in length and 90 kg in weight.

> ★ STAR FACT ★
> *Nothosaurus* had nostrils on the top of its snouts, which suggests that it came to the water's surface to breathe, like crocodiles.

- **Nothosaurs emerged** in the middle of the Triassic Period (250–208 mya), but were extinct by the end of it.

- **The place left** by the extinct nothosaurs was taken by the plesiosaurs – another group of marine reptiles, but ones that were better adapted to life in the seas.

◄ *Nothosaurus was an aquatic reptile that could use its webbed feet to move over land. The long-necked nothosaurs may be ancestors of plesiosaurs.*

Ichthyosaurs

- **Ichthyosaurs** looked similar to sharks, which are fish, and to the later dolphins, which are mammals. When one type of animal evolves to look like another, scientists call it convergence.

- **Unlike plesiosaurs**, which relied on their paddles to propel them forwards, ichthyosaurs swayed their tails from side to side, like fish.

- **Hundreds of complete skeletons** of the ichthyosaur *Ichthyosaurus* have been discovered. This reptile could grow up to 2 m long, and weighed 90 kg.

- *Ichthyosaurus* had large ear bones, which it may have used to pick up underwater vibrations caused by prey.

- **Some fossilized skeletons** of *Ichthyosaurus* and other ichthyosaurs have embryos (unborn infants) inside. This shows that ichthyosaurs gave birth to live young, as opposed to laying eggs.

> ★ STAR FACT ★
> The first *Ichthyosaurus* fossil was found in 1811 by the English fossil-hunter Mary Anning. It took seven years before scientists identified the skeleton as that of a reptile.

- **One of the largest ichthyosaurs** was *Shonisaurus*, which was 15 m long and weighed 15 tonnes.

- **Ichthyosaurs were plentiful** in the Triassic and Jurassic Periods (250–144 mya), but became rarer in the Late Jurassic and in the Cretaceous Periods (144–65 mya).

- **Ichthyosaur means** 'fish lizard'.

- **Fossil-hunters have found** ichthyosaur remains all over the world – in North and South America, Europe, Russia, India and Australia.

◄ *Fossils of prehistoric marine reptiles such as Ichthyosaurus created a sensation in the early 19th century because fossil hunters discovered them before they had found any dinosaur remains.*

Plesiosaurs

● **Plesiosaurs** were marine reptiles that lived from the Late Triassic to the Late Cretaceous Periods (215–80 mya).

● **They were better suited** to marine life than nothosaurs or placodonts. Their limbs were like paddles, which moved their bodies through water.

● **Many plesiosaurs** had long necks, small heads, strong jaws and sharp teeth.

● **The diet** included fish, squid and pterosaurs (flying reptiles), which flew above the water.

● **The first** Plesiosaurus **fossil** was discovered at Lyme Regis, England in the 19th century. The fossil is 2.3 m long.

● **Plesiosaurus** was not a fast swimmer. It used its flipper-like limbs to move through the water but it had a weak tail that could not propel it forward very powerfully.

● **Elasmosaurus**, the longest plesiosaur, lived in the Cretaceous Period (144–65 mya). It grew up to 14 m long and weighed up to 3 tonnes.

● **One group of plesiosaurs** were known as pliosaurs. They had shorter necks, much larger heads and huge jaws and teeth.

● **Research suggests** that plesiosaurs may have caught prey with quick, darting head movements.

▼ Elasmosaurus had a 5 metre-long neck— as long as three people lying head to toe.

> ★ STAR FACT ★
> One large pliosaur was Rhomaleosaurus, another was Liopleurodon. Both could grow up to 15 m long.

Pteranodon

Mosasaurs

● **Mosasaurs** were a group of large sea reptiles. They first between 160 and 120 mya.

● **Mosasaurs were diapsid reptiles,** which included dinosaurs and pterosaurs. Other large sea reptiles belonged to the euryapsids group.

● **Mosasaurs** have living relatives. These include monitor lizards, such as the Komodo dragon.

● **The best-known mosasaur** is *Mosasaurus*, which could be up to 10 m long and 10 tonnes in weight.

● **The teeth of *Mosasaurus*** were cone-shaped, each with different cutting and crushing edges. They were the most advanced teeth of any sea reptile.

● **So distinctive are *Mosasaurus'* teeth** that palaeontologists have identified its tooth marks on fossils of the giant turtle *Allopleuron*.

◀ *Mosasaurus was a fast swimmer. It had an enormous tail and huge paddle-shaped limbs.*

● **The jaws of a *Mosasaurus*** were found in a mine in Maastricht, the Netherlands, in 1780. The fossil disappeared in 1795 when France invaded, but turned up in Paris.

● **Scientists first thought** the jaws were from a prehistoric whale or crocodile, not a giant lizard.

● ***Mosasaurus* means** 'lizard from the River Meuse', as it was found in Maastricht, through which the river Meuse flows.

● **In 1998,** more than 200 years after the discovery of the first *Mosasaurus* fossil, palaeontologists found the remains of another *Mosasaurus* in the same location – St Pietersburg quarry in Maastricht.

Rhamphorhynchoids

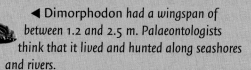

◀ Dimorphodon *had a wingspan of between 1.2 and 2.5 m. Palaeontologists think that it lived and hunted along seashores and rivers.*

● **The earliest pterosaurs** (flying reptiles) were the rhamphorhynchoids. They first appeared in the Late Triassic Period (around 220 mya).

● **Rhamphorhynchoids** had long tails that ended in a diamond-shaped vane, like a rudder.

● **Their tails** gave them stability in flight, which meant they could soar and swoop effectively.

● **One of the first** rhamphorhynchoids – and first flying vertebrates – was *Peteinosaurus*.

● **Well-preserved fossils** of *Peteinosaurus* have been found near Bergamo in Italy.

★ **STAR FACT** ★
Fossil-hunters have found *Rhamphorhynchus* fossils alongside those of the early bird *Archaeopteryx*, in Solnhofen, Germany.

● **They reveal *Peteinosaurus'* sharp**, cone-like teeth, and suggest it ate insects, which it caught in the air.

● **In contrast**, another early rhamphorhynchoid, *Eudimorphodon*, had fangs at the front of its mouth and smaller spiked ones behind. This suggests that it ate fish.

● ***Dimorphodon*** was a later rhamphorhynchoid from the Early Jurassic Period (208–180 mya). It had a huge head that looked a bit like a puffin's.

● **One of the last** rhamphorhynchoids to appear was *Rhamphorhynchus*, in the Late Jurassic Period (160 mya).

Pterodactyls

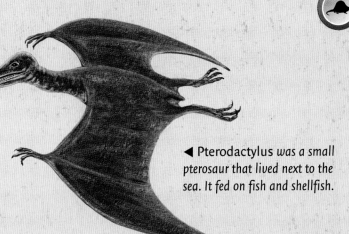

- **Pterodactyls** are a later group of pterosaurs (flying reptiles) than the rhamphorhynchoids.

- **They lived in the Late Jurassic** through to the Late Cretaceous Periods (160–65 mya).

- **Pterodactyls** lacked the long, stabilizing tail of rhamphorhynchoids, but were more effective fliers, able to make quicker turns in the air.

- **They were also much lighter** than rhamphorhynchoids, because their bones were hollow.

- **The pterodactyl** *Pterodactylus* and the rhamphorhynchoid *Rhamphorhynchus* were roughly the same size, but *Pterodactylus* weighed between 1 and 5 kg, while *Rhamphorhynchus* weighed 10 kg.

- **Some of the largest pterodactyls,** such as *Pteranodon*, appeared in the Late Cretaceous Period and had a wingspan of 7 m.

- **Unlike earlier flying reptiles,** *Pteranodon* had no teeth. Instead, it used its long, thin beak to scoop up fish.

◀ *Pterodactylus was a small pterosaur that lived next to the sea. It fed on fish and shellfish.*

- **Pteranodon also had** a pelican-like pouch at the bottom of its mouth – it probably used this to store fish before swallowing them.

- **Pteranodon weighed about 16 kg**. This was heavier than earlier pterodactyls, and suggests it was probably a glider rather than an active flyer.

- **Pteranodon** had a long crest on its head, which may have worked as a rudder during flight.

Quetzalcoatlus

- *Quetzalcoatlus* was the largest known flying animal of any kind ever to have lived.

- **It had a wingspan** of 15 m – the size of a small aeroplane!

- **It was also the heaviest flying reptile,** weighing 86 kg. Its bulk suggests that it was not a brilliant flyer, and instead glided as much as possible.

- **Its name comes from** an Aztec word meaning 'feathered serpent'. Quetzalcoatl was the Aztec god of death and resurrection.

- *Quetzalcoatlus* had long, narrow wings, jaws without teeth, and a long, stiff neck.

◀ *Quetzalcoatlus belonged to a family of pterosaurs called the azhdarchids, which had giant wingspans, long necks and toothless beaks. The name 'azhdarchid' comes from the Uzbek word for a dragon.*

- **Palaeontologists** were amazed when they discovered the fossil bones of *Quetzalcoatlus* – they did not think a flying creature could be that large.

- **The discovery of these bones** in inland areas, suggests *Quetzalcoatlus* may have flown over deserts like a vulture.

- **Some palaeontologists** say that *Quetzalcoatlus* was not like a vulture as its beak was not designed for ripping at the bodies of dead animals.

- **Another puzzle** is how *Quetzalcoatlus* could lift itself off the ground to fly.

★ STAR FACT ★
A student, Douglas Lawson, discovered *Quetzalcoatlus*' bones in the Big Bend National Park, Texas, in 1971.

Flight

▶ Birds' skeletons, such as this modern-day pigeon's, are built for flight. The bones are lightweight and often hollow, the finger bones in the wing are joined to provide greater strength and the ribs, backbone and breastbone form a secure cage that supports powerful wings.

- **Pterosaurs** (flying reptiles) evolved wings that consisted of a stretched membrane (a piece of thin skin).

- **The fourth finger** of flying reptiles was extremely long, and held up the wing membrane.

- **Flying reptiles** had an extra flap of skin, between the shoulder and wrist, that gave added stability in flight.

- **The forelimbs grew longer** and developed into wings.

- **They also developed feathers**, which possibly evolved from the scales of their reptile ancestors.

- **Flying birds have asymmetrical feathers**, with longer barbs on one side of the shaft than the other. This helps to lift them up and allows them to fly. Flightless birds have symmetrical feathers – which is why they cannot fly.

- **One theory** of how birds and reptiles developed flight is that as they ran along the ground, they flapped their arms to give them stability. Over time, these arms developed into wings.

- **Another theory** is that some animals glided between trees searching of food. They then developed wings.

- **Feathered bird wings** survive injury better than the more fragile skin wings of flying reptiles could have done. This may suggest why birds have outlived pterosaurs.

> ★ STAR FACT ★
> The reason why palaeontologists are confident that *Archaeopteryx*, the first known bird, could fly is because it had asymmetrical feathers.

Archaeopteryx

◀ Archaeopteryx is the first known flying bird, but it would not have been a very efficient flyer because of its primitive skeleton and long tail.

- *Archaeopteryx* is the earliest known flying bird.

- **It lived** in the Late Jurassic Period (159–144 mya).

- **Roughly** the size of a magpie – it would have weighed about 270 g and had a wingspan of approximately 60 cm.

- **Probably eight identified** *Archaeopteryx* fossils have been found, ranging from almost a whole skeleton to just one feather, all of them preserved in limestone, in Solnhofen, southern Germany.

> ★ STAR FACT ★
> The chick of the hoatzin bird, which lives in Venezuela and Guyana, has claws on each wing that are very similar to *Archaeopteryx*'s. It uses them to climb and cling onto trees.

- **The fossils reveal** that *Archaeopteryx* had feathers and that, like modern birds, they were asymmetrical – one side was thicker than the other.

- *Archaeopteryx* **was therefore capable of flight**, but could not fly long distances as it lacked a suitable skeleton.

- **Like carnivorous dinosaurs**, *Archaeopteryx* had jaws with teeth, and forelimbs that had separate fingers with claws.

- *Archaeopteryx* **looks so similar** to a small dinosaur that one museum labelled its *Archaeopteryx* fossil as such for decades until someone realized it had feathers.

- *Archaeopteryx* **was a tree-dwelling creature.** The big toe at the end of its hind legs pointed backwards, allowing it to grip branches.

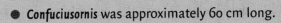

Confuciusornis

- **Confuciusornis** was the first-known bird to have a true birdlike beak.

- **It lived** in the Late Jurassic to Early Cretaceous Periods (around 150–120 mya).

- **Unlike the slightly older** *Archaeopteryx*, which had a mouth filled with teeth, *Confuciusornis*, had a toothless beak, like modern birds.

- **This beak had an upwards curve** – a fact that has led palaeontologists to argue about this bird's diet. Some think it ate seeds and others that it hunted fish.

▶ A *male Confuciusornis. Scientists think that males had long tail feathers, but females had much shorter tails.*

- **Confuciusornis** was approximately 60 cm long.

- **It had lightweight bones**, a deep chest and a short, rudder-like tail. All of this means it was probably a better flyer than *Archaeopteryx*.

- **Like** *Archaeopteryx*, it had a backwards-pointing big toe on its hind feet, which suggests it lived in trees.

- **The remains of** *Confuciusornis* were discovered at the Liaoning Fossil Beds, in northeast China, in the mid 1990s.

- **The Liaoning Fossil Beds** were the site of a prehistoric lake. Fossil-hunters have found so many *Confuciusornis* fossils at this site that the bird probably lived in large colonies on the lakeshore.

- **Confuciusornis** means 'Confucius bird'. It is named after the ancient Chinese philosopher Confucius.

Terror birds

- **After the dinosaurs** became extinct (about 65 mya), huge flightless birds – known as terror birds – seized the opportunity to become the dominant predators of their day.

- *Gastornis* was one such terror bird. It had an enormous head and powerful legs, like those of its dinosaur ancestors, so it could outrun its prey.

- **Some experts believe** that *Gastornis* is the ancestor of ducks, geese and other related birds.

- **Even though these birds were huge**, they were quick light-footed runners as they had hollow bones.

- **The diets of terror birds** included small and medium-sized mammals, such as rodents and horses.

- **During the Late Eocene** and Oligocene Epochs (40–24 mya), big carnivorous mammals became more powerful and better hunters and so more dominant, taking over.

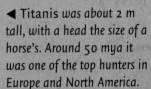

◀ *Titanis was about 2 m tall, with a head the size of a horse's. Around 50 mya it was one of the top hunters in Europe and North America.*

- **However, in South America**, which was cut off from North America and the rest of the world for much of the Tertiary Period (65–1.6 mya), terror birds managed to stay dominant for longer.

- **One South American terror bird** was *Phorusrhacus*, which grew up to 1.5 m tall.

- **Titanis was another** South American terror bird, and the biggest of all – it was 2.5 m tall and weighed 150 kg.

- **Unlike other flightless birds** *Titanis* had clawed fingers ar the end of its fore-limbs.. It probably used these for seizing its prey.

Other flightless birds

● **Most prehistoric flightless birds** were giants, but not
all of them were terror birds.

● *Shuvuuia*, which lived about 80 mya, was an early,
flightless bird. Like the terror birds, it was very large.

● *Shuvuuia* **was about 1 m high.** It probably fed on insects
and small reptiles.

● **The name** *Shuvuuia* comes from the Mongolian word for
'bird'. It lived on the plains of Central Asia and had the
long, thin legs of a fast runner.

● **For a long time**, palaeontologists thought that
Shuvuuia was a reptile, but in fact its skull is much more
similar to a modern bird's than a reptile's.

● **Much later giant birds** grew to incredible sizes. Dinornis
was the tallest flightless bird ever at 3.5 m tall.

▶ These living
flightless birds
are descendants
of prehistoric
flightless birds.
The collective
name for
flightless birds
is ratites.

Cassowary

Kiwi

● **Dinornis lived in New Zealand.** It first appeared about
2 mya and survived until 300 years ago!

● **At 450 kg,** *Aepyornis* was the heaviest bird ever to have
lived. It lived on the island of Madagascar between
2 million and 500 years ago.

● **Both** *Dinornis* **and** *Aepyornis* were herbivores. Their diet
consisted of seeds and fruit.

Water birds

● *Ichthyornis* was a prehistoric seagull, which first
appeared in the Late Cretaceous Period (85–65 mya).

● **It was similar in size** to a modern seagull, but had
a much larger head and a beak full of very sharp teeth.

● *Presbyornis* was a prehistoric duck. Like *Ichthyornis*,
it evolved in the Late Cretaceous Period and was abundant
in the Early Tertiary Period (65–40 mya).

● *Presbyornis* **was much bigger** than a modern duck –
it stood between 0.5 m and 1.5 m tall.

● **It had much longer legs** than its modern relative and
so may have been a wading bird rather than a diving bird.

● *Presbyornis* **lived** in large flocks on lake shores, like
modern flamingos.

▶ Some experts believe that
Palaelodus was a prehistoric flamingo
that lived in France about 26 mya.

● **Osteodontornis was a huge flying**
bird, with a wingspan up to 5.2 m
across.

● **It lived in the Miocene Epoch**
(24–5 mya), and would have flown
over the North Pacific Ocean.

● *Osteodontornis* had a long bill,
lined with toothlike bony spikes.
Its diet probably included squid,
seized from the surface of the sea.

Land birds

▶ Parrot fossils date back to at least 20 mya.

● **Land birds** are flying birds that fly in the skies over land and hunt or feed on the ground, unlike water birds.

● **Fossils of prehistoric land birds** are rare because their bones were light and would not have fossilized well.

● **As a result**, there are big gaps in palaeontologists' knowledge of the evolution of many species of birds. However, there are some species they do know about.

● *Archaeopsittacus* was an early parrot of the Late Oligocene Epoch (28–24 mya).

● *Ogygoptynx* was the first-known owl. It lived in the Palaeocene Epoch (65–58 mya).

● *Aegialornis* **lived** in the Eocene and Oligocene Epochs (58–24 mya). It may be the ancestor of swifts and hummingbirds.

● *Gallinuloides* was an early member of the chicken family. Fossils have been found in Wyoming, USA, in rock strata of the Eocene Epoch (58–37 mya).

● **The earliest-known vultures** lived in the Palaeocene Epoch (65–58 mya).

● **The earliest-known hawks**, cranes, bustards, cuckoos and songbirds lived in the Eocene Epoch.

★ STAR FACT ★
Neocathartes was an early vulture-like bird. There are similarities between its skeleton and that of storks, which suggests vultures and storks are closely related.

Argentavis

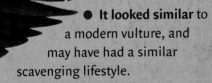

▶ The colossal *Argentavis*, whose fossils were discovered in 1979, is an ancestor of North American turkey vultures.

● *Argentavis* was an enormous bird of prey – the largest one ever discovered.

● **Its wingspan** was more than 7 m across, which is double the size of the largest modern living bird, the wandering albatross.

● **Individual** *Argentavis* feathers were up to 1.5 m long!

● *Argentavis* **lived** between 8 and 6 mya.

● **It looked similar** to a modern vulture, and may have had a similar scavenging lifestyle.

● **Its huge size and weight** (up to 80 kg) suggests that it was more of a glider than an active flier.

● *Argentavis* **was possibly bald-headed**, with a ruff of feathers around its neck, much like a modern vulture or a condor.

● **It had a large, hooked beak,** which was probably more effective at grabbing hold of prey than its feet.

● *Argentavis* **means** 'bird of Argentina' and it is so-called because its remains were first discovered there.

● *Argentavis* **belonged** to a family of extinct flying birds called teratorns.

Rise of the mammals

- **The earliest mammals** were small, shrewlike creatures that appeared in the Late Triassic Period (220–208 mya).

- **After their initial emergence,** mammals developed little in the two periods following the Triassic, Jurassic and Cretaceous Periods (208–65 mya).

- **This is because dinosaurs dominated the land** at this time. Mammals had to remain small and hidden to avoid becoming prey.

- **It was only after dinosaurs became extinct** around 65 mya, that mammals started to evolve into larger and more varied forms.

- **Mammals (and birds)** have bigger brains than reptiles, and are also warm-blooded.

- **These abilities meant** that mammals could be adaptable – something that ensured their success in the changing climates of the Tertiary and Quaternary Periods (65 mya to the present).

- **The rise of mammals** to the top was not instant – during the Early Tertiary Period, (65–58 mya), the major killers were the giant flightless terror birds.

- **During the Eocene Epoch,** (58–37 mya), mammals became the most dominant animals on land.

- **Eocene mammals** also took to the air in the form of bats – and the seas in the form of whales – and later, dolphins and seals.

- **Mammals have been** – and still are – the most adaptable of all backboned animals.

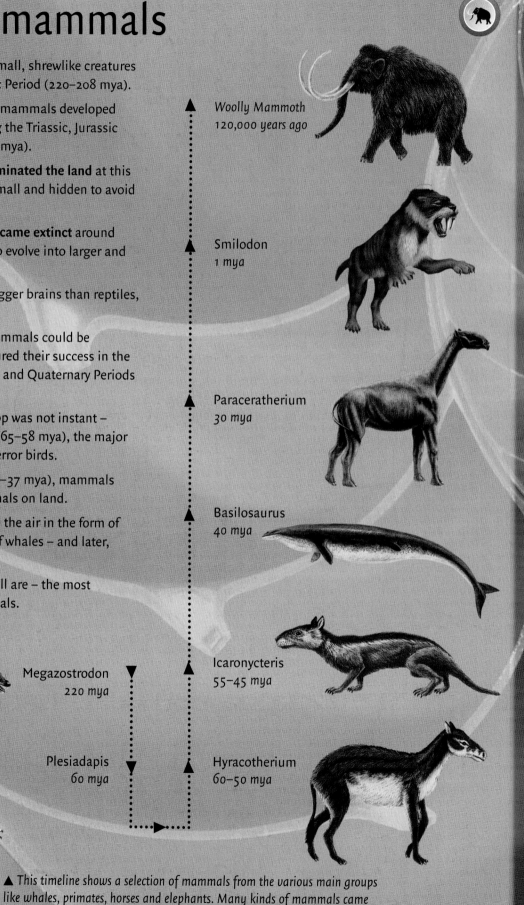

Woolly Mammoth
120,000 years ago

Smilodon
1 mya

Paraceratherium
30 mya

Basilosaurus
40 mya

Icaronycteris
55–45 mya

Hyracotherium
60–50 mya

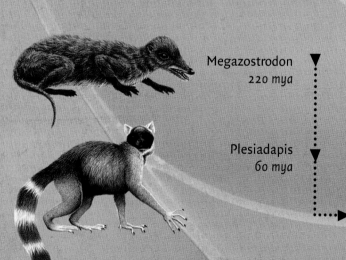

Megazostrodon
220 mya

Plesiadapis
60 mya

▲ This timeline shows a selection of mammals from the various main groups like whales, primates, horses and elephants. Many kinds of mammals came and went during prehistory, and the ones that are alive today are a relatively limited selection of all the mammals that have ever existed on Earth.

Early mammals

- *Megazostrodon* was one of the first true mammals. It appeared at the end of the Triassic Period (about 220 mya).

- **It was a shrewlike insectivore** (insect-eater) and about 12 cm long. It had a long body that was lo_ the ground and long limbs that it held out to the side squatting position.

- *Eozostrodon* was another very early mammal, which emerged about the same time as *Megazostrodon*.

- **It had true mammalian teeth**, including two different sorts of cheek teeth – premolars and molars – which were replaced only once during its lifetime.

- **Its sharp teeth suggest** it was a meateater, and its large eyes suggest that it hunted at night.

- **A further early mammal** was *Morganucodon*. It too had premolars and molars and chewed its food in a roundabout motion, rather than the up-down motion of reptiles.

▲ Like other small, early mammals, Megazostrodon *was probably a nocturnal animal, coming out to hunt at night.*

- *Sinoconodon* was another early mammal that lived in the Early Jurassic Period (about 200 mya).

- **These early mammals** also had three middle ear bones, which made their hearing more sensitive than reptiles.

- **They also had whiskers**, which suggests they had fur, which in turn suggests they were warm-blooded.

- **All mammals** are warm-blooded, which means they maintain a constant body temperature. Fur helps some mammals to keep warm – at night, for instance.

Offspring

- **Mammals developed** a different way of producing young, compared to reptiles and birds, which lay eggs.

- **Instead, most mammals are viviparous**, which means they give birth to live young.

- **One mammal group**, the monotremes, defies this rule by laying eggs. There are five surviving monotremes – the duck-billed platypus and four species of echidna.

- **After the young of mammals are born**, their mothers feed them milk, produced in their mammary glands.

- **The word 'mammal'** comes from the mammary glands – the part of female mammals' bodies that secretes milk.

- **The first mammals**, such as *Megazostrodon*, *Eozostrodon* and *Morganucodon* grew a single set of milk teeth, which suggests that the young fed on breast milk.

- **Milk teeth are temporary teeth** that grow using the nutrients provided by milk, and prepare the jaw for later teeth.

- **Mammals can be divided** into three groups depending on how they rear their young – placentals, marsupials and monotremes.

- **In placental mammals**, the offspring stays inside its mother's body, in the womb, until it is a fully developed baby – at which point it is born.

- **Marsupial mammals give birth** to their offspring at a much earlier stage. The tiny infants then develop fully in their mothers' pouch, called a marsupium.

◄ Marsupial mammals, such as this kangaroo and its joey (infant), give birth at an earlier stage than other mammals.

Rodents

- **In terms of numbers**, variety and distribution, rodents are the most successful mammals that have ever lived.

- **Squirrels**, rats, guinea pigs, beavers, porcupines, voles, gophers and mice are all types of rodent.

- **Rodents have been** – and still are – so successful because they are small, fast-breeding and able to digest all kinds of foods, including substances as hard as wood.

- **The first-known rodent** was *Paramys*, which appeared about 60 mya.

- *Paramys* **was a squirrel-like rodent** that could climb trees. It was 60 cm long, and had a long, slightly bushy tail.

- **Modern squirrels evolved** from *Paramys* 38 mya. These mammals have one of the longest ancestries we know of.

▶ Platypittamys *was a prehistoric, ratlike rodent. Rodents became plentiful during the Oligocene Epoch (37–24 mya).*

- **Another early rodent** was *Epigaulus*, which was a gopher with two horns.

- *Epigaulus* **was 26 cm long** and lived in North America in the Miocene Epoch (24–5 mya). It probably used its horns for defence or digging up roots.

- **Prehistoric rodents could be massive**. *Castoroides* was an early beaver that was over 2 m long – almost the size of a black bear.

> ★ STAR FACT ★
> Rabbits and hares are descended from rodents. Modern hares first appeared around 5 mya.

Carnivores

- **The first carnivorous mammals** ranged in size from the catlike *Oxyaena* to the wolflike *Mesonyx*.

- **In the Late Eocene Epoch** (around 40 mya) large carnivores appeared, such as *Andrewsarchus*.

- **Modern carnivores** are descended from a separate group called miacids.

- **Carnivores belong** to the order Carnivora. This order had two subgroups – the fissipeds, which include the cat and dog families and the pinnipeds (seals, sea lions and walruses). Many classification schemes put pinnipeds in their own group, separate from fissiped carnivores.

▶ Potamotherium *was a carnivore, very similar to modern-day otters. It hunted fish in rivers and streams.*

> ★ STAR FACT ★
> Allodesmus was a prehistoric seal. It had flippers, large eyes and spiky teeth, which it used to impale slippery fish.

- **During the Oligocene Epoch** (37–24 mya), fissipeds began to replace creodonts as the dominant carnivores.

  - **Fissipeds** were smart, fast, and deadly. They were the only predators that could catch fast-running herbivores.

  - **Faster mammals evolved** in the Oligocene Epoch as forests changed to open woodlands, with more space to run after, and from, other creatures.

  - **Carnivores gradually developed** bigger brains, more alert senses, sharper claws and teeth, and stronger jaws and limbs.

  - **Pinnipeds** are carnivorous mammals that, like whales and dolphins, reinvaded the seas.

Herbivores

● **The first specialist herbivores** (plant eaters) appeared in the Late Palaeocene Epoch (around 60 mya).

● **They ranged in size** from the equivalent of modern badgers to pigs.

● **These herbivores** foraged for food on forest floors.

● **It was not until** the very end of the Palaeocene Epoch (58 mya) that the first large herbivores evolved.

● **Large herbivores emerged** before large carnivores. They must have had a peaceful life – for a while!

● **Uintatherium was a large early herbivore.** It was the size of a large rhinoceros.

● **Uintatherium had three pairs of** bony knobs protruding from its head. Males had long, strong canine teeth, which they used if attacked.

● **The growth of grasslands** and the decline of forests in the Miocene Epoch (24–5 mya) speeded up changes to herbivores' bodies.

● **They could** outrun carnivores in open spaces. They also developed better digestive systems to cope with the new, tough grasses.

● **The most important requirements** for a herbivore are complex teeth and digestive systems to break down plant food and release its energy.

◄ A mother Uintatherium and her baby. This strange-looking creature was the largest land animal of its time. Its head was covered in horns and it had small tusks.

Cats

★ STAR FACT ★
Prehistoric cats' ability to unsheathe and retract their claws provided them with one of their deadliest weapons – and one that cats still have.

● **Cats are the fastest** most intelligent hunters, with the sharpest claws and teeth.

● **Cats evolved along two lines.** One extinct group is the sabre-tooths, which included *Smilodon*.

● **Sabre-tooths preyed on** large, heavily-built animals with thick hides, which explains their long canine teeth.

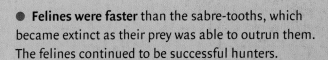

● **The other group of cats** is the felines, which are the ancestors of modern cats, from lions to pet cat.

● **Felines were faster** than the sabre-tooths, which became extinct as their prey was able to outrun them. The felines continued to be successful hunters.

● **One prehistoric feline** was *Dinictis*, a puma-sized cat that lived in the Oligocene Epoch (37–24 mya).

● **A later feline** was *Dinofelis*, which lived between 5 and 1.4 mya.

● *Dinofelis* means 'terrible cat'. It , had strong front legs that it used to press down on its prey before stabbing with its teeth.

● **Dinofelis' diet** included baboons, antelope and australopithecines – our human ancestors.

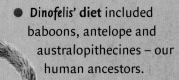

◄ Dinictis was a fissiped carnivore and member of the cat family, which lived about 30 mya.

Dogs

- **Early dogs hunted** in a similar way to modern wild dogs – in packs.

- **Dogs developed long snouts**, which gave them a keen sense of smell, and forward-pointing eyes, which gave them good vision.

- **Dogs also developed a mixture of teeth** – sharp canines for stabbing, narrow cheek teeth for slicing and, farther along the jaw, flatter teeth for crushing.

- **These different teeth** meant that dogs could eat a variety of different foods, including plants, which they might have had to eat if meat was in short supply.

▶ A pack of Hesperocyon dogs, tracking the scent of their prey. Organized hunting is an example of dogs' intelligence.

★ STAR FACT ★
Hunting in packs allowed *Hesperocyon* to catch large animals that it would not have been able to kill on its own.

- **One of the ancestors of dogs**, as well as bears, was the bear-dog *Amphicyon*. Its name means 'in-between dog'. It lived between 40 and 9 mya.

- **Fossils footprints of *Amphicyon*** show that it walked like a bear with feet flat on the ground.

- ***Hesperocyon*** was an early dog, living between 37 and 29 mya.

- ***Hesperocyon* was the size of a small fox.** It had long legs and jaws, forward-pointing eyes and a supple, slender body.

Andrewsarchus

- ***Andrewsarchus*** is one of the largest meat-eating land mammals that has ever existed.

- **It lived in Asia** in the Late Eocene Epoch (around 40 mya).

- **No complete *Andrewsarchus* skeleton** has ever been found – only its skull, which measured 83 cm long.

- **Palaeontologists have built up** an impression of the rest of the animal's body from knowledge of its skull, and its relation to the earlier, bearlike *Mesonyx*.

- **If their impression is correct**, *Andrewsarchus* was 5 m long.

- **It had long, strong jaws**, which it used to eat a variety of foods.

- ***Andrewsarchus* was a scavenger** and an omnivore.

- **It belonged to a group** of mammals known as mesonychids.

- **Fossil-hunters have found** most mesonychid remains near prehistoric rivers and coasts, suggesting that this was where they lived and hunted.

★ STAR FACT ★
Andrewsarchus means 'Andrew's flesh-eater'. It was named after the naturalist, explorer and writer Roy Chapman Andrews (1884–1960).

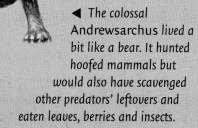

◀ The colossal Andrewsarchus lived a bit like a bear. It hunted hoofed mammals but would also have scavenged other predators' leftovers and eaten leaves, berries and insects.

Smilodon

- **Smilodon** was a terrifying predator that belonged to a group of cats called sabre-tooths.

- **It lived between** 1 million and 11,000 years ago in North and South America.

- **One of Smilodon's most distinctive features** was its huge, curved canine teeth, which could be up to 25 cm long. It could also open its jaws to an angle of about 90 degrees!

- **The first sabre-tooth** was *Megantereon*. It lived about 30 mya.

- **Smilodon was only a little larger** than a big lion, but was around twice its weight at 200 kg.

- **Its 'design' was more like a bear's** than a modern cat's – it had very powerful forelegs, a thick neck, and a short spine.

- **Because of its shorter spine** and heavier build, *Smilodon* was not as fast as feline cats (the ancestors of modern cats). But it made up for this with its power and its teeth.

- **Smilodon preyed on** large and slow-moving creatures, such as prehistoric bison, mammoths, giant camels and ground sloths.

- **Smilodon was a top predator**, with no real enemies and no direct competitors – until the emergence of modern humans.

▼ Smilodon *was a fearsome predator. It became extinct because it was not fast enough to catch the quick-running mammals that evolved at the end of the last ice age, about 11,000 years ago.*

★ **STAR FACT** ★

Smilodon's large canines were very delicate. They could break when stabbing thick-skinned animals, such as bison.

Paraceratherium

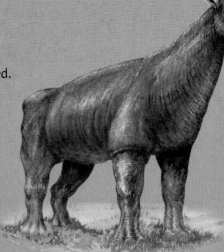

- **Paraceratherium** is the largest land mammal to have lived.

- **It was a gentle giant**, which could be as tall as 5.5 m at the shoulder.

- **Paraceratherium belonged** to the group of mammals called perissodactyls – hoofed mammals with an odd number of toes.

- **It was also an early rhinoceros**, but unlike its living relatives, had no horns on its snout.

- **Remains of this huge beast** have been discovered in Europe and Central Asia, where it lived between 30 and 16 mya.

- **Until recently** this beast was known as *Indricotherium*, but it is now more commonly known as *Paraceratherium*.

- **Paraceratherium** had long front legs and a long neck, which it used like a giraffe to reach leaves on the high branches of trees.

◄ *Also known as Indricotherium, Paraceratherium was a giant, long-necked rhinoceros. Although it was massively heavy, long legs indicate that Paraceratherium was capable of running.*

- **Males were larger than females,** and had heavier heads with more dome-shaped skulls.

- **In comparison with the rest of its body,** *Paraceratherium*'s skull was quite small.

> ★ **STAR FACT** ★
> Male *Paraceratherium* could be as heavy as 30 tonnes – four times the weight of a modern elephant!

Megatherium

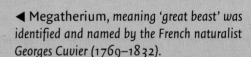

- **Megatherium** was a giant ground sloth – an extinct type of sloth that lived about 5 mya.

- **Megatherium was** 7 m tall. It had strong arms and massive claws, which it used to pull down branches and uproot trees.

- **It had short hind legs** and a powerful tail that it used for extra support when it stood up on its rear legs to reach the tallest branches.

- **Megatherium walked** on its knuckles on its forelimbs and on the side of its feet on its hind legs.

- **The size of *Megatherium*** would have put off predators, but it also had very tough skin as extra defence.

- **The remains of ground sloth skin** found in caves in South America show that its was made even stronger by tiny lumps of bone.

◄ *Megatherium, meaning 'great beast' was identified and named by the French naturalist Georges Cuvier (1769–1832).*

- **Megatherium lived in parts of South America,** such as present-day Bolivia and Peru.

- **When South America became joined** to North America about 3 mya, *Megatherium* spread northwards.

- **Megatherium is thought to have become extinct** 11,000 years ago, but some people in Argentina claim it lived until 400 years ago. If so, it is likely that humans killed off the last of these giants.

> ★ **STAR FACT** ★
> *Megatherium* belonged to a group of mammals called edentates, which lacked front teeth.

Glyptodonts

▶ Glyptodon, means 'grooved tooth'. It was named by the English scientist Richard Owen (1804–1892) from fossilized bones that the English naturalist Charles Darwin (1809–1882) brought back with him from South America.

● **Glyptodonts** were giant armadillos that lived in South America between 5 million and 11,000 years ago.

● **They had domelike shells** and armoured tails that ended in a spiked club.

● **Their tail also served** as an extra support when they reared up on their hind legs – either to defend themselves against attackers or to mate.

● **They also had powerful jaws** and huge cheek teeth that were constantly replaced, unlike most other mammals.

★ STAR FACT ★
Glyptodonts' armour and tails were similar to those of ankylosaur dinosaurs. This is another example of evolutionary convergence – when separate groups of animals develop similar characteristics.

● **This meant** that glyptodonts could chew through the toughest plants without wearing down their teeth.

● **Glyptodon was a 3 m-long glyptodont.** Like other glyptodonts it did not have front teeth.

● **Doedicurus was an even bigger glyptodont.** It weighed 1400 kg and was 4 m long – the size of a big car!

● **Doedicurus is** the most heavily-armoured planteater ever to have lived. A sledgehammer would have made little impression on its massive, bony shell.

● **The body armour and weaponry** of glyptodonts were designed to protect them against predators such as Thylacosmilus (see pages 154–155).

Bats

★ STAR FACT ★
Bats are the only mammals that are known to have reached Australia after it became isolated from the rest of the world around 40 mya.

● **Icaronycteris** is the earliest-known bat. Its fossil remains are between 55 and 45 million years old.

● **Despite its age,** Icaronycteris looked similar to a modern bat. It had large ears, which it may used as a sonar, like modern bats.

● **One difference from modern bats** was that Icaronycteris' tail was not joined to its legs by flaps of skin.

● **Palaeontologists think** that there must have been earlier, more primitive-looking bats from which Icaronycteris evolved.

● **The chance of finding** earlier prehistoric bat fossils is very small – like birds, bats have very fragile skeletons that do not fossilize well.

● **Icaronycteris ate insects.** Palaeontologists know this because they have found insect remains in the part of the fossil where its stomach would have been.

● **Icaronycteris fossils** have been found in North America.

● **The fossil remains** of another prehistoric bat, Palaeochiropteryx, have been found in Europe.

● **Like Icaronycteris,** this bat seems to have been an insectivore (insect eater).

◀ Like this living bat, prehistoric bats such as Icaronycteris probably used sonar to sense nearby objects and hunt for prey. Bats use sonar by making a high-pitched sound and then listening to its echoes.

Marsupials

- **Marsupials** are mammals that give birth to offspring at an early stage in their development – when they are tiny.

- **After being born**, the infant crawls through its mother's fur to a pouch called the marsupium, where it stays, feeding on milk, until it is big enough to leave.

- **The first marsupials** probably evolved in North America and then spread to South America and Australia.

- *Alphadon*, meaning 'first tooth', was an early marsupial that emerged 70 mya. It lived in North and South America.

- *Alphadon* **was 30 cm long** and weighed 300 gm. It would have lived in trees, using its feet to climb and fed on insects, fruit and small vertebrates.

- **When Australia became isolated** from the rest of the world about 40 mya, its marsupials continued to evolve – unlike the rest of the world, where they died out.

◄ Procoptodon *was a giant kangaroo about 3 m tall. In Australia, marsupials such as kangaroos occupied the position taken by hoofed mammals in other parts of the world.*

- **Marsupials continued** to exist in South America, which was also isolated from the rest of the world, during much of the Tertiary Period (65–1.6 mya).

- **But when South America** became reconnected with North America, about 3 mya, the arrival of placental mammals from the north led many marsupials to become extinct.

- **Today, there are only two** surviving groups of marsupials in the Americas: the opossums found throughout America and the rat opossums found in South America.

- Australia has many living marsupials, from kangaroos to koalas. However it had a much greater marsupial population in the Tertiary Period – we know this from fossil sites such as Riversleigh in northwest Queensland.

Thylacosmilus

- *Thylacosmilus* was a carnivorous marsupial. It belonged to a family of South American marsupials called the Borhyaenidae, all of whom had large skulls and teeth.

- **It lived and hunted** on the grassy plains of South America in the Pliocene Epoch (5–1.6 mya).

- *Thylacosmilus* **was about** the size of a modern jaguar, growing up to 1.2 m long and weighing about 115 kg.

- **There are some amazing similarities** between *Thylacosmilus* and the sabre-tooth cats, such as *Smilodon*.

- *Thylacosmilus* **also had** long, upper canine teeth, which it used to stab its prey.

- **Like** *Smilodon*, *Thylacosmilus* had powerful shoulder and neck muscles, and it could press its huge canines down with great force.

- **This is remarkable** as the sabre-tooths were placental mammals that evolved in North America and *Thylacosmilus* was a marsupial that evolved in South America at a time when the two continents were not connected.

- **It is example** of evolutionary convergence – when separate animal groups develop similar characteristics.

- **The teeth of** *Thylacosmilus*' grew throughout its life.

- *Thylacosmilus* **became extinct** after the land bridge between North and South America was re-established. It could not compete with the more powerful carnivores that arrived from the north.

◄ Thylacosmilus *had much in common with sabre-tooth cats, but it had some differences too. Unlike true cats, it was a marsupial, its teeth never stopped growing and it could not retract its claws.*

Elephant evolution

- **Elephants and their ancestors** belong to an order of animals called Proboscidea, meaning 'long-snouted'.

- **The ancestors of elephants** appeared around 40 mya. They were trunkless and looked a bit like large pigs.

- **Moeritherium** is the earliest known ancestor. It is named after Lake Moeris in Egypt, where its fossils were found.

- **It was 3 m long** and weighed 200 kg, and probably spent much of its life in rivers or lakes, like a hippo.

- **The next step in the development** of elephants was taken by *Phiomia*, which lived about 36 mya.

- **Phiomia had a trunk** as well as two pairs of tusks.

- **Phiomia is the first-known** of a group of elephants called mastodonts. Its shoulder height was up to 2.4 m.

- **One group of elephants** that descended from *Phiomia* were the deinotheres, which had one pair of enormous downward curving tusks in the lower jaw.

- **Other groups that evolved** from mastodonts were true elephants (resembling living elephants) and mammoths, which appeared in the Pliocene Epoch (5–1.6 mya).

◄ The hippopotamus-like Moeritherium. *The American palaeontologist Henry Fairfield Osborn (1857–1935) described it as 'a missing link' between elephants and other mammals.*

Platybelodon

▶ It was thought Platybelodon *ate soft water plants. Recent research on its fossilized tusks suggests that it ate tougher plant material.*

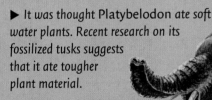

- **Platybelodon** was an early – but not the first – member of a group of prehistoric elephants called mastodonts.

- **It lived about 25 mya** in the cold northern regions of Europe, Asia and North America.

- **Platybelodon's lower jaw** ended in two very wide, flat tusks – like a pair of spades.

- **Platybelodon is called** 'shovel-tusker', because palaeontologists think it used its tusks as a shovel to scoop up plants.

- **It also had flat cheek teeth**, sharp front teeth, and a very wide trunk.

- **This mastodont** had a pair of tusks on its upper jaw, too. They slotted into an indentation near the top of its lower tusks when the mouth was closed.

- **Platybelodon** weighed between 4 and 5 tonnes.

- **The time period** in which *Platybelodon* lived was quite short compared to other animals, and other species of elephant in particular.

- **This is because** *Platybelodon* was a specialized feeder and vulnerable to any climate change that would affect the plants it ate.

Woolly mammoth

- **Woolly mammoths** (scientific name *Mammuthus primigenius*) lived between 120,000 and 6000 years ago.

- **They lived on the steppes of Russia and Asia** and the plains of North America during the ice ages of the Quaternary Period (1.6 mya to the present).

- **To survive these cold places**, woolly mammoths were designed for warmth and insulation.

- **Their woolly coats** were made up of two layers of hair – an outside layer of long, coarse hairs, and a second layer of densely packed bristles.

- **They also had very tough skins** – up to 2.5 cm thick – beneath which was a deep layer of fat.

★ STAR FACT ★
People often think the woolly mammoth had red hair, but in fact this colour was a chemical reaction that happened after the animal died.

- **Male woolly mammoths** could grow up to 3.5 m long and 2.9 m high at the shoulder, and weigh up to 2.75 tonnes.

- **They had long tusks** that curved forward, up and then back. They used their tusks to defend themselves against attackers and – probably – to clear snow and ice to reach low-lying plants.

- **Some cave paintings** by Cro-Magnon humans clearly depict woolly mammoths.

- **Many excellently preserved woolly mammoth** remains have been discovered in the permanently frozen ground of Siberia.

▼ In 1994, scientists discovered DNA, or genetic material, in the fossil remains of a woolly mammoth. They found that it was nearly identical to the DNA of living elephants.

Columbian mammoth

- **The Columbian mammoth** (scientific name *Mammuthus columbi*) was an even bigger than the woolly mammoth.

- **Its coat was not thick** like the woolly mammoth's, and it lived in warm areas, such as North America and Mexico.

- **The Columbian mammoth grew** up to 4.2 m high at the shoulder, and weighed over 10 tonnes – the equivalent of 130 adult humans!

- **It ate more than** 350 kg of food and drank about 160 litres of water each day.

- **It used its trunk** for feeding, as well as for moving and breaking things.

- **This trunk was like an extra arm.** It had two finger-like projections at the end, which could grab hold of objects.

- **Its tusks grew** up to 5 m long. It used these for fighting rival mammoths and defending itself against predators.

- **Some scientists think** the Columbian mammoth was the same species as the imperial mammoth (scientific name *Mammuthus imperator*). The imperial mammoth was one of the largest mammoths to have lived, estimated to have stood 4.8 m high at the shoulder.

- **Both the Columbian** and the imperial mammoths lacked thick coats and lived in relatively warm climates.

- **The imperial mammoth's tusks** were much more twisted than those of the Columbian mammoth.

◄ *Early humans hunted the Columbian mammoth, a fact known from finds of tools and building materials made out of the mammoth's bone.*

The first horses

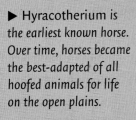

▶ *Hyracotherium is the earliest known horse. Over time, horses became the best-adapted of all hoofed animals for life on the open plains.*

- **Horses** have one of the best fossil records of any animal, so palaeontologists have been able to trace their evolution from the earliest horselike mammals to the modern horse.

- **Hyracotherium is the first-known horse.** It lived in forests in North America and Europe in the Late Palaeocene and Early Eocene Epochs (60–50 mya).

- **Another name for Hyracotherium** is *Eohippus*, which means 'dawn horse'.

- **Hyracotherium was the size of a fox.** It had a short neck, a long tail and slender limbs. It also had three toes on its hind feet and four toes on its front feet.

- **Mesohippus** was one of the next horses to evolve after *Hyracotherium*, between 40 and 25 mya. Its name means 'middle horse'.

- **Mesohippus had longer legs** than *Hyracotherium* and would have been a faster runner.

- **It would also have been** better at chewing food, because its teeth had a larger surface area.

- **An improved chewing ability** was important for horses and other plant-eaters as forests gave way to grasslands, and more abundant but tougher plants.

- **Mesohippus had also evolved** three toes on its front feet to match the three on its hind feet.

- **As horses evolved,** they migrated from North America and Europe to Asia, Africa and South America.

Later horses

- **Merychippus** lived between 11 and 5 mya. It was the size of a pony.

- **It was the first horse** to eat only grass, and – to help it reach the grass – had a longer neck and muzzle (snout) than earlier horses.

- **Merychippus' middle toe** had also evolved into a hoof, although this hoof did not have a pad on the bottom, unlike modern horses.

- **The legs** were designed for outrunning carnivores. Its upper leg bones were shorter than previous horses, the lower leg bones were longer.

- **Shorter upper leg bones** meant that the horse's main leg-moving muscles could be packed in at the top of the leg – which translates into a faster-running animal.

- **Hipparion**, which means 'better horse', was a further advance on *Merychippus*. It had thinner legs and more horse-like hooves.

- **Hipparion lived** between 15 and 2 mya.

◀ The pony-sized Hypohippus lived around the same time as Merychippus, between 17 and 11 mya. Unlike later horses it had three spreading toes, which helped it walk on the soft ground of the forests where it lived.

- **Pliohippus** was an even more advanced horse. The side toes that *Hipparion* still had, had vanished on *Pliohippus*, making it the first one-toed horse.

- **Pliohippus' teeth** were similar to those of modern horses – they were long and had an uneven surface for grinding up grass.

- **Equus**, the modern horse and the latest stage in the evolution of the animal, first appeared around 2 mya.

Whales

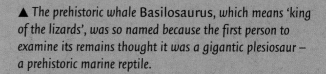

- **Basilosaurus** which first appeared about 40 mya, closely resembled whales we are familiar with today, more so than its ancestors *Pakicetus* and *Ambulocetus*.

- **It was also enormous!** It measured between 20 and 25 m long – the same as three elephants standing in a row.

- **It had a variety of teeth** in its mouth – sharp teeth at the front for stabbing, and saw-edged teeth at the back for chewing.

- **Basilosaurus ate large fish**, squid, and other marine mammals.

- **There were some big differences** between *Basilosaurus* and modern whales. For a start, it had a slimmer body.

- **It also lacked a blowhole**, a nostril on the top of modern whales' heads that they breathe out of when they come to the surface. Instead, *Basilosaurus* had nostrils on its snout.

- **Prosqualodon did have a blowhole** and was a more advanced whale than *Basilosaurus*. It lived between 30 and 20 mya.

▲ The prehistoric whale Basilosaurus, which means 'king of the lizards', was so named because the first person to examine its remains thought it was a gigantic plesiosaur – a prehistoric marine reptile.

- **It may have been the ancestor** of toothed whales, a group that includes sperm whales, killer whales, beaked whales and dolphins.

- **Prosqualodon looked similar** to a dolphin. It had a long, streamlined body and a long, narrow snout, which was full of pointed teeth.

> ★ STAR FACT ★
> *Cetotherium* was a prehistoric baleen whale that first appeared 15 mya. Instead of teeth, these whales had hard plates in their mouths called baleen that filtered plankton and small fish.

The first whales

● **The very first whales** looked nothing like the enormous creatures that swim in our oceans today.

● *Ambulocetus*, one of the first members of the whale family, looked more like a giant otter. It lived about 50 mya.

● **Ambulocetus means** 'walking whale', and it spent more time on land than in water.

● **It would, however**, have been a good swimmer. Fossil remains show that *Ambulocetus* had webbed feet and hands.

● **An even earlier whale ancestor** than *Ambulocetus* was *Pakicetus*, which lived about 52 mya.

● *Pakicetus* is named after the country Pakistan, where a fossil of its skull was found in 1979.

● *Pakicetus* **was around** 1.8 m long. *Ambulocetus*, at 3 m, was bigger.

● **Palaeontologists think** that whales evolved from carnivorous hoofed mammals called mesonychids.

● **Around 40 mya**, the first true whales, which swam only, evolved from their half-walking, half-swimming ancestors.

> ★ STAR FACT ★
> Only the back of *Pakicetus*' skull and part of its lower jaw have been found. From this, however, palaeontologists can tell it was not able to dive very deeply.

▼ *Pakicetus could run and swim well. It probably lived alongside rivers and streams and hunted animals both in and out of the water.*

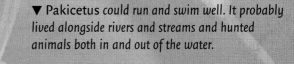

Megaloceros

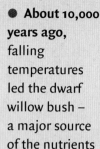

▶ *Scientists used to believe that, because Megaloceros' antlers were so big, they could only have been used for display purposes – to scare off rivals. In the 1980s however, research proved that these antlers were used for fighting.*

● **Megaloceros** is one of the largest species of deer ever to have lived. Adult males were 2.2 m long, 2 m tall at the shoulders and weighed 700 kg.

● **It lived** between 400,000 and 9000 years ago.

● **Megaloceros is known as** the Irish elk as a large number of its fossils have been found in Ireland in peat bogs.

● **Megaloceros lived all over Europe**, the Middle East, China and North America, too.

● **It had a broader**, flatter snout than modern deer, which suggests it was a less fussy eater and just ate plant food in huge quantities.

● **Like modern deer**, *Megaloceros* males shed their antlers and grew another pair every year. For antlers as big as *Megaloceros'*, this required a huge intake of nutrients.

● **About 10,000 years ago,** falling temperatures led the dwarf willow bush – a major source of the nutrients *Megaloceros* needed to grow its antlers – to decline.

● **This food shortage** is one theory as to why *Megaloceros* became extinct.

● **Another theory is** that early humans, who greatly prized *Megaloceros'* antlers, hunted it to extinction.

> ★ **STAR FACT** ★
> *Megaloceros* was a fast runner – it could move at around 80 km/h. It used this turn of speed to escape from predators such as wolves.

Early primates

▶ *The early primate Plesiadapis had a long tail and claws on its fingers and toes – unlike later monkeys and apes, which had nails.*

● **The primates** are a group of mammals that include lemurs, monkeys, apes and humans.

● **Primates have a much greater range** of movement in their arms, legs, fingers and toes than other mammals.

● **They also have a more acute sense of touch** because their fingers and toes end in flat nails, not curved claws – so the skin on the other side evolved into a sensitive pad.

● **The ancestors of primates** were small insectivorous (insect-eating) mammals that looked like shrews.

● **The first known primate** was *Plesiadapis*, which lived about 60 mya in Europe and North America. It was a squirrel-like tree climber.

● **More advanced primates** developed about 10 million years later. They looked a bit like modern lemurs.

● **Notharctus** was one of these lemur-like primates. It ate leaves and fruit, was about 40 cm long, and had a grasping thumb to grip well to branches.

● **More advanced** primates include *Smilodectes* and *Tetonius*. They had larger brains and eyes and longer tails than *Plesiadapis*.

● **These animals were ancestors** of tarsiers, lemurs and lorises, but not higher primates – the monkeys, apes and humans.

● **One early monkey** was *Mesopithecus*, which lived 8 mya. It was similar to modern monkeys, but had a longer tail.

Apes

▼ The early ape Dryopithecus stood about 1 m tall. It had the largest brain for its size of any mammal and flourished in open grassland regions in Africa, Asia and Europe.

● **Dryopithecus was a chimp-like ape** that evolved after Proconsul and lived in the Miocene Epoch (24–5 mya). It may have stood on two legs but climbed using all four.

● **Ramapithecus was an ape** that lived in the Middle and Late Miocene Epoch. It is now thought to be part of the chain of evolution of Asian apes and is possibly an ancestor of the orang-utan.

● **Australopithecines** were a further step in the evolution from apes to humans. Australopithecines (meaning 'southern apes') walked on two legs.

● **The biggest-ever ape** was Gigantopithecus, which lived in China until around 1 mya. It may have been up to 2.5 m tall and weighed 300 kg.

> ★ STAR FACT ★
> Proconsul was named in 1927 after Consul, a performing chimpanzee that appeared on stage smoking a pipe and riding a bicycle.

● **Apes are primates** that have more complex brains than monkeys and no tails. Hominids (early humans) evolved from apes.

● **Aegyptopithecus** was one of the ancestors of apes. It lived in Egypt in the Oligocene Epoch (37–24 mya). It was small and had a short tail.

● **Proconsul**, which lived between 23 and 14 mya, was an early ape. Its body size varied from that of a small monkey to that of a female gorilla, and had a larger brain than Aegyptopithecus.

● **Proconsul was a fruit eater.** Palaeontologists think that it walked on four limbs with part of its weight supported by the knuckles of its hands, like modern chimpanzees and gorillas.

● **Two lines of apes developed** after Proconsul. From one line came gibbons and orang-utans, from the other chimpanzees, gorillas and humans.

▶ The enormous Gigantopithecus could probably stand on its hind legs to reach food.

Walking upright

- **Hominidae** is the human family of ourselves, our ancestors and prehistoric relatives.
- **Hominid fossils** demonstrate their evolution from apes that walked on all fours.
- **Hominid spines** developed an S-shaped curve so that the hips supported the weight of the upper body.
- **Hominid heads** evolved to sit on top of the spine, while apes' heads sit at the front.

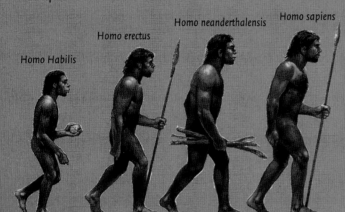

Homo Habilis

Homo erectus

Homo neanderthalensis

Homo sapiens

> **★ STAR FACT ★**
> The first fossilized footprints of an upright walker were discovered in 1978. They belong to *Australopithecus afarensis*, which lived 3.8 mya.

- **Hominids' have** flat feet to support the body on the ground. Apes have curved toes for climbing.
- **Hominid leg bones** became longer and straighter than those of apes, so they could walk greater distances.
- **Walking on two legs** helped hominids cover greater distances in the open grasslands of Africa.
- **It also let them** to see above tall grasses, an advantage when looking for food or keeping a lookout for danger.
- **Upright walking** freed the arms to do other things, such as carrying babies or food.

◀ *Walking upright was one of the most important developments in the history of hominids.*

Offspring

- **Human parents** look after their young for a longer period than any other animal.
- **A close bond** between parents and young is also a feature of modern primates – and would have been for prehistoric primates, too.
- **This is because humans and primates** have small numbers of infants compared to many other animals, and females are pregnant for longer.
- **There is also a longer period** of upbringing during which time offspring learn survival and social skills.
- **The pelvises of early hominids** were wide, which meant that their offspring were quite large when they were born.
- **Like modern humans**, later hominids – from *Homo ergaster* on – had smaller pelvises, which meant that their babies were smaller and less developed when born.

◀ *A female orang-utan and infant. Primates have closer relationships with their young than other animals. Unlike monkeys and apes, human babies cannot move around independently after birth and are very dependent on their mothers.*

- **Smaller and less developed babies** require more care and protection – as a result, childcare became an even bigger concern for hominids.
- **This change led to other ones.** Hominid groups increased in size, so that the responsibility for childcare could be spread.
- **There was also more cooperation** between males and females and they began to pair-up in partnerships.
- **Such partnerships** were mutually beneficial – the female could look after the offspring while the male provided food. In turn, the male could be certain that the offspring was his own.

Early hominids

● **One of the earliest-known** hominids (early humans) is *Ardipithecus ramidus*, which lived about 4.5 mya.

● **It would have looked similar** to a chimpanzee except for one major difference, *Ardipithecus ramidus* walked on two legs.

● **It lived in woods**, sleeping in trees at night, but foraging on the ground for roots during the day.

● **An adult *Ardipithecus ramidus* male** was about 1.3 m tall and 27 g in weight.

● **Archaeologists discovered** the teeth, skull and arm fossils of *Ardipithecus ramidus* in Ethiopia in 1994.

● **In 2001,** archaeologists in Ethiopia found the remains of an even older hominid, *Ardipithecus ramidus kadabba*, which lived between 5.6 and 5.8 mya.

◀ *Ardipithecus ramidus. Scientists gave it its name from the Afar language of Ethiopia – 'ardi' means 'ground' while 'ramid' means 'root' – words that express its position at the base of human history.*

● **The fossils of *Ardipithecus ramidus kadabba*** are similar to those of *Ardipithecus ramidus*, so it is possible both are closely related.

● **Some scientists argue,** however, that *Ardipithecus ramidus kadabba* is closer to an ape than a hominid.

● **Australopithecus anamensis** is a later hominid. Its fossils date to between 4.2 and 3.9 million years old.

● **A fossil of one of *Australopithecus anamensis*' knee-joints** shows that it shifted its weight from one leg to the other when it moved – a sure sign that it walked on two legs.

Sahelanthropus tchadensis

● **In 2002,** French archaeologists announced the discovery of a new species called *Sahelanthropus tchadensis*. It may be a missing link between apes and early hominids.

● **The archaeologists discovered** a near-complete fossil skull of *Sahelanthropus tchadensis*, which has been dated to between 7 and 6 million years old.

● **They also found the fossils** of two pieces of jawbone and three teeth.

● **The French team** found the skull not in East Africa, like all the other early hominids, but in Chad, central Africa.

● **Finding the skull in Chad** indicates that early hominids ranged well beyond East Africa, where scientists previously believed all early hominids lived.

● **The skull was nicknamed** *Toumaï*, meaning 'hope of life' in Goran, an African language.

● **Despite its great age**, *Sahelanthropus tchadensis*' skull suggests that it had a surprisingly human face, which protruded less than apes.

▶ *The skull of Sahelanthropus tchadensis. Some people believe that this is the remains of the oldest hominid of all.*

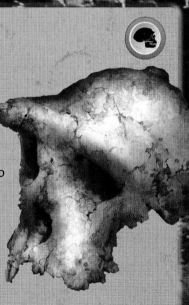

● *Sahelanthropus tchadensis* also had heavy ridges for its eyebrows. Some archaeologists believe that, because of this, it was closer to an ape than a hominid, since female apes have similar heavy ridges.

● **Like later hominids**, *Sahelanthropus tchadensis* had small canine teeth and did not grind its teeth in the same way as apes.

● *Sahelanthropus tchadensis* lived alongside a diverse range of animals. Other fossil finds in the same region include more than 700 types of fish, crocodiles and rodents.

Australopithecus afarensis

- **Australopithecus afarensis** was an early hominid that lived 3.5 mya.

- **Its brain** was the size of a modern chimpanzee's, and it had the short legs and long arms of modern apes.

- **Australopithecus afarensis was** 90 to 120 cm in height.

- **Like other australopithecines**, it walked on two legs. This was the most efficient way for it to move in search of food.

- **It had a wider pelvis** and shorter legs than modern humans. This may have made it a more efficient walker than modern humans.

- **Australopithecus afarensis ate seeds**, fruits, nuts and occasionally meat.

- **These hominids had a brief childhood,** reaching adulthood at the age of 11 years old. They lived for a maximum of 50 years.

◀ Australopithecus afarensis spent its days on the ground, foraging for food, but at night may have slept in trees.

- **Fossil footprints of Australopithecus afarensis** show that their feet were similar to ours.

- **The first fossils of Australopithecus afarensis** to be discovered belonged to a female. They were found in 1974, at Hadar in Ethiopia.

★ STAR FACT ★

Johanson and Gray named the female 'Lucy' after the Beatles' song 'Lucy in the Sky with Diamonds', which they listened to on the day of their discovery.

Homo habilis

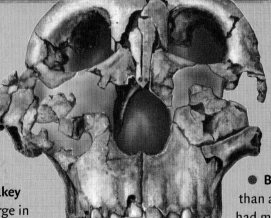

- **Homo habilis** is one of the earliest-known members of the genus Homo, to which we also belong.

- **Homo habilis lived** between 2.4 and 1.6 mya.

- **The archaeologists Louis and Mary Leakey** first discovered its remains at Olduvai Gorge in Tanzania, in 1961.

- **Fossils of Homo habilis' skulls** have since been found around Lake Turkana in Kenya, one of the richest sites for hominid fossils in the world.

- **The skulls show** that Homo habilis had a flat face with prominent cheekbones, similar to australopithecines, which it would have lived alongside.

- **Homo habilis was much more ape-like** than its successor, Homo ergaster. It had fur and lacked any form of language.

◀ The first Homo habilis skull found by Louis and Mary Leakey in Tanzania. Homo habilis had a bigger brain than any previous hominid.

- **But it did have a bigger brain** than any australopithecine. It also had more flexible hands and straighter, more sensitive fingers.

- **Homo habilis means 'handy man'** – it could use its hands to gather fruit and crack nuts. It also created the first stone tools.

- **A fully grown Homo habilis male** was around 1.5 m tall and weighed about 50 kg.

★ STAR FACT ★

Homo habilis used stone tools to crack open animal bones so it could eat the nutritious marrow inside.

Homo ergaster

● **Homo ergaster** was the first 'human-looking' early human. It first appeared about 1.9 mya.

● **Adult males** grew to approximately 170 cm tall, with long, slender limbs and a straight spine.

● **Homo ergaster was the first** smooth-skinned hominid, unlike its hairy ancestors. Like us it cooled down by sweating, not panting, which is how earlier hominids cooled themselves.

● **It was also the first hominid** to have a protruding nose – previous hominids merely had nostrils on the surface of their face.

● **Homo ergaster was generally** a scavenger, although it would hunt and kill older or weaker animals.

● **Scientists know that it ate a lot of meat** because one of the skeletons that have been found shows evidence of a bone disease caused by eating too many animal livers.

● **Fossil remains of Homo ergaster** were first discovered in 1975. The most complete skeleton was found in 1984.

● **The skeleton belonged to a teenage boy** named Nariokotome Boy after the site in Lake Turkana, Kenya, where it was found.

● **The structure of Nariokotome Boy's bones** suggest that he was much stronger than modern humans.

● **Homo ergaster was the first hominid** to travel beyond Africa. One place where its remains have been found is Dmanisi, in the Republic of Georgia, near Russia.

▼ Homo ergaster *was different from any previous hominid. It was taller, with a face that was more lightly built and had smaller cheek teeth.*

Homo erectus

● **Homo erectus** may be a descendant of *Homo ergaster*.

● **It was almost identical** to its immediate ancestor, except that it had thicker skull bones and a more protruding eyebrow ridge.

● **Homo erectus and Homo ergaster** lived alongside each other for 2 million years.

● **While Homo ergaster became extinct** about 600,000 years ago, *Homo erectus* survived until less than 50,000 years ago.

● **Like its ancestor**, *Homo erectus* spread beyond Africa and settled in Europe and Asia.

● **In the 19th century**, Eugène Dubois found *Homo erectus* fossils on the island of Java. He was a palaeoanthropologist (someone who studies hominid fossils).

● **In the 1930s**, archaeologists discovered more than 40 *Homo erectus* skeletons in China.

◄ *Stone hearths in caves that were used by Homo erectus prove that it had mastered fire. Fire provided warmth, light, protection and the means to cook food.*

● **The archaeologists also found evidence** that *Homo erectus* used fire and practised cannibalism!

● **For a long time,** people called the human to which the Chinese fossils belonged 'Peking Man'. It was much later that palaeoanthropologists realized it was, in fact, *Homo erectus*.

★ **STAR FACT** ★
The 'Peking Man' fossils disappeared at the beginning of the World War II and have never been found. They were confiscated by Japanese troops just when they were about to be shipped to the USA.

Homo heidelbergensis

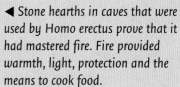

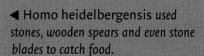

● **Homo heidelbergensis** lived between 600,000 and 250,000 years ago in Africa and Europe.

● **It was the first hominid** to settle in northern Europe.

● **Homo heidelbergensis** had a body like ours, but it had a heavier jaw, a flat nose and thick eyebrow ridges.

● **The teeth of Homo heidelbergensis** were 50 percent longer than ours.

● **They also had a thicker covering of enamel,** which suggests that it ate tough animal flesh and maybe used its teeth for gripping objects.

● **Towards the end of its existence,** *Homo heidelbergensis* would have lived alongside Neanderthals.

● **Homo heidelbergensis** is named after the city of Heidelberg in Germany. It was near there that one of the hominid's jawbones was found in 1907.

◄ *Homo heidelbergensis used stones, wooden spears and even stone blades to catch food.*

● **The greatest find of Homo heidelbergensis' fossils** was made in the Atapuerca hills of northern Spain, in 1976. Archaeologists discovered the remains of 32 individuals.

● **In the mid 1990s,** archaeologists unearthed *Homo heidelbergensis* bones, tools and animal carcasses in England. The carcasses had been stripped of their meat.

★ **STAR FACT** ★
Unlike the Neanderthals that came later, there is no evidence that *Homo heidelbergensis* buried its dead.

Homo neanderthalensis

● **Homo neanderthalensis** – or Neanderthals – lived between 230,000 and 28,000 years ago across Europe, Russia and parts of the Middle East.

● **Homo neanderthalensis means** 'man from the Neander Valley', which is the site in Germany where the first of its fossil remains were found in 1865.

● **Neanderthals are our extinct cousins** rather than our direct ancestors .

● **They were about 30 percent heavier** than modern humans.

● **Neanderthals' shorter, stockier bodies** were suited to life in Europe and Russia during the ice ages of the Pleistocene Epoch (1.6 million to 10,000 years ago).

> ★ **STAR FACT** ★
> Many people think that Neanderthals were slow and stupid, but in fact their brains were at least as big as modern human's.

● **They had sloping foreheads** and heavy brow ridges.

● **They buried their dead,** cooked meat and made tools

● **Neanderthals made the first spears** tipped with stone blades.

● **For about 10,000 years** Neanderthals lived beside modern humans in Europe, before becoming extinct.

◄ *Early humans had to face many natural dangers, such as cave bears.*

Homo floresiensis

● **In 2004**, Australian palaeoanthropologists discovered a new species of human, *Homo floresiensis*, which lived on the Indonesian island of Flores between 95,000 and 13,000 years ago.

● **The remains of seven** specimens have been found.

● **The most complete** skeleton is that of a female. Study of of its leg bone shows that it walked upright.

● **Before the discovery** it was thought *Homo sapiens* had been the sole remaining human species since the disappearance of Neanderthals 30,000 years ago.

● **Palaeoanthropologists nicknamed** *Homo floresiensis* 'hobbit man' because of its tiny size. It was about one metre tall.

● **Its small brain size** does not seem to have reflected its intelligence – *Homo floresiensis* was a skilled toolmaker.

● **Flores, off the coast of Asia**, has been an island for over a million years. Being small represents an adaptation to living on an island, where resources were limited.

◄ *Two Homo floresiensis hunters prepare to attack a pygmy elephant. The discovery of this new species of human challenges our ideas of human evolution.*

● **Some people believe** that this human species evolved into a smaller creature to cope with its island habitat.

● **Local people** have told stories of little hairy people, *ebu gogo*, meaning 'grandmother who eats anything'.

● **Homo floresiensis was a hunter.** It preyed on the pygmy elephant. Both *Homo floresiensis* and the pygmy elephant seem to have become extinct after a volcanic eruption 12,000 years ago.

Homo sapiens

- **Homo sapiens** means 'wise man'. They appeared in Africa 150,000 years ago. Humans belong to this species.

- **The first Homo sapiens** outside Africa appeared in Israel, 90,000 years ago.

- **By 40,000 years ago,** *Homo sapiens* had spread to many parts of the world.

- **The humans** that settled in Europe are Cro-Magnons. They dressed in furs and hunted with spears and nets.

- **Cro-Magnons** had a basic language and culture, which included wall paintings.

- **They were similar to modern humans,** but with slightly bigger jaws and noses and more rounded braincases.

◀ *Cave painting, cooking and toolmaking are all features of early Homo sapiens. They different from other human species, having a higher forehead and a more prominent chin.*

- **Homo sapiens probably arrived** in North America about 30,000 years ago.

- **They would have crossed the Bering land bridge** – formed by shrunken sea levels – from present-day Siberia to present-day Alaska.

- **The earliest-known human culture** in North America is that of the Clovis people, which is thought to be 11,500 years old.

- **Modern humans have** evolved only slightly from the earliest Homo sapiens.

Brains and intelligence

- **Primates,** from which hominids descended, had bigger brains in relation to body size than other mammals.

- **Primates developed larger brains** – and more intelligence – as living in trees required balance, coordination and skilful use of hands and feet.

- **Once hominids' brains started getting bigger,** their skulls began to change. Bigger brains led to the development of foreheads.

- **Homo habilis' brain** was 50 percent bigger than its predecessors, with a capacity of 750 ml.

- **Its brain structure** was different to that of earlier hominids. It had bigger frontal lobes – parts of the brain linked to problem-solving.

- **Homo habilis used its greater intelligence** find meat, which it scavenged from animals kills.

- **Meat gave hominids** bigger brains. Breaking down plant food uses lots of energy. Eating fewer plants allowed more energy for the brain.

- *Homo ergaster* **had an even bigger brain,** with a capacity of around 1000 ml. It used its intelligence to read animal tracks – a key development in hunting.

- The brain of *Homo erectus* became larger during its existence. About 1 mya its brain capacity was 1000 ml; 500,000 years later it was 1300 ml.

- Our brain capacity is 1750 ml.

Australopithecus afarensis

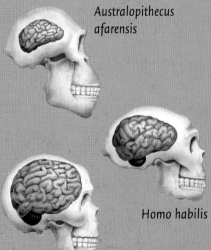

Homo habilis

Homo sapien

◀ *Brain size is linked to intelligence, but what makes humans and our ancestors intelligent is our brain's complex structure.*

Tools

- **The greatest number** of *Homo habilis* tools has been found in the Olduvai Gorge in Tanzania. They include rocks that were used as hammers, flakers, choppers and scrapers.

Stone tool

- **Homo habilis used** these tools to cut meat and, especially, to scrape open animal bones to eat the marrow inside.

- **The stone tools** used by *Homo habilis* are crude and basic. This hominid was the first toolmaker, but, hardly surprisingly, it was not a skilled one.

- **But making these early stone tools** was still a challenging task – the toolmaker needed to strike one rock with another so that it would produce a single, sharp flake rather than shattering into many pieces.

- **Toolmaking requires considerable intelligence.** It involves the use of memory, as well as the ability to plan ahead and to solve abstract problems.

- **Homo ergaster's tools** were more advanced. It made tear-drop shaped, symmetrical hand axes called 'Acheulean axes', after the place in France where similar axes have been discovered from a later period.

- **Neanderthals made** sharp flakes of stone, called Levallois flakes, which were placed on the end of spears.

- **This method required** great precision and dexterity. While modern humans have a broader range of skills, they would be hard pushed to make such tools.

- **Modern humans developed** the greatest variety of tools. Cro-Magnon tools include knives, spearpoints and engraving tools.

- **Cro-Magnon humans** also began to make tools from materials other than stone, including wood, bones, antlers and ivory.

Hunting

- **Homo erectus** was one of the earliest human hunters. Earlier hominids may have hunted small or lame animals, but mainly scavenged other animals' kills.

- **Homo erectus** drove animals into traps using fire. They made handaxes to kill animals or butcher them once dead.

- **The Neanderthals** excelled at hunting – a skill they developed during the ice ages of the Pleistocene Epoch (1.6–0.01 mya).

- **Hunting developed** not only provided food, but also clothing and materials for tools.

- **Neanderthals used nets or spears** to catch fish. They also hunted seals.

- **In the 1990s,** finds of Neanderthal weapons in England showed the range of its hunting tools. They include axes, knives, and blades.

- **As well as hunting meat,** hominids gathered fruits, vegetables and nuts.

- **Another Neanderthal site,** at Schöningen in Germany, had the remains of nine polished wooden spears, made from a spruce tree.

- **Each spear** was over 2 m long, and was designed to be thrown like a javelin.

- **Homo sapiens developed new weapons** for hunting, including the bow and arrow, the blowpipe and the boomerang.

◄ *Early humans developed more sophisticated methods of hunting, including weapons, traps and fire.*

INDEX